CAGE AND AVIARY SERIES

FOREIGN BIRDS –
EXHIBITION AND MANAGEMENT

OTHER BOOKS AVAILABLE

Cage Bird Hybrids
V.A.V. Carr

Guide to Cage Birds
David Alderton

The Border Canary
Joe Bracegirdle

The Gloster Fancy Canary
John S. Cross

The Yorkshire Canary
Ernest Howson

World of Budgerigars
C.H. Rogers

Ornamental Waterfowl
A.A. Johnson and W.H. Payn

Exhibition and Flying Pigeons
Harry G. Wheeler

Pheasants and Their Enemies
James O'C Fitzsimons

Bantams for Everyone
H. Easom Smith

FOREIGN BIRDS

EXHIBITION AND MANAGEMENT

By

James Buchan

With Colour Plates by
Michael Stringer

Published by
SAIGA PUBLISHING CO. LTD.,
1 Royal Parade, Hindhead, Surrey
GU26 6TD England

© JAMES BUCHAN and SAIGA PUBLISHING, 1981

ISBN 0 86230 039 8

This book is copyright and may not be reproduced in whole *or in part* (except for review) without the express permission of the publishers in writing.

DEDICATION

TO MY CHILDREN — GILLIAN, EWAN AND STUART

SF
461
.B91

Typeset by Inforum Ltd, Portsmouth
Printed and bound in Great Britain by
Whitstable Litho Ltd, Whitstable, Kent

Published by
SAIGA PUBLISHING CO. LTD.
1 Royal Parade, Hindhead, Surrey,
GU26 6TD England

Contents

MONOCHROME ILLUSTRATION LIST

LIST OF COLOURED PLATES

Acknowledgements

Acknowledgement, for their kind help in providing black and white photographs, is due to:
Mr H.V. Lacey for the Paradise Whydah (5.4), White Javas (3.5), Purple Glossy Starling (2.10), Necklace Dove (4.4), Mexican Green Jay (2.11) and European Waxwing (7.3).
The Editor of *Cage and Aviary Birds* for the views of the 1980 National Exhibition of Cage and Aviary Birds (figures 8.5, 8.7, 10.1, 10.4).
All the drawings are taken from old books: *Foreign Birds for Cage and Aviary* (Parts I and II), *Practical Bird-Keeping, Favourite Foreign Birds*, *Bird Notes* Vol. III.

Note: These drawings do not necessarily represent the present-day exhibition specimens, as certain features tend to be over-emphasised for artistic effect. However, they remain useful for identifying the different species.

The remaining black and white illustrations and photographs were provided by the author.

PREFACE

It is well over a quarter of a century since I acquired my first exotic birds, while I was still a schoolboy, and I can still recall the wonder and pride which those Silverbills and Orange-cheeked Waxbills elicited. Today, even the acquisition of a much-coveted species can scarcely recreate the emotions which I experienced then as a complete novice.

When talking to those who have just obtained their first birds, or are about to do so, I am often conscious of the fact that it is easy to forget just how rudimentary our knowledge of aviculture was in the beginning. Matters which the experienced fancier takes for granted with scarcely a thought, are often a closed book or source of confusion to the novice.

Although there are many volumes dealing with the various aspects of foreign species in the field and in confinement, I do not know of any book which covers the subject of exhibiting in detail.

For this reason I have attempted to describe the whole process of Foreign Bird exhibiting in as much detail as the limits of this volume will permit. The experienced exhibitor will find much that is basic, but I hope that the novice, and the newcomer to this fascinating pastime, will be provided with all the information required to enable him to exhibit his birds with confidence.

JAMES BUCHAN

Coleford,
Gloucestershire.

CHAPTER 1

Show Species I Parrot-Like and Common Seedeaters

BASIC FACTORS GOVERNING CHOICE

The main problem for the novice will be in buying the correct species for exhibiting. Although almost any species may be exhibited, with the stipulated exception of all of the Birds of Prey, the choice will be governed by personal resources, preference and experience. Initially, the beginner should commence with some of the hardier, common seedeaters and, as he gains experience, progress to rarer species.

The range of foreign birds which generally appear on the show bench can be sub-divided into three very broad categories:

1. **Seedeaters (Finches, Buntings, etc.)**
2. **Parrot-like (Short-tailed Parrots, Love birds, etc.)**
3. **Softbills (All Insectivorous, Fruit-eating and Nectar-feeding species).**

As more knowledge and experience is acquired, the fancier may decide to specialise in one of these categories or even in a subdivision of one, for example Australian Finches or Tanagers. Alternatively, he may wish to build up a show team covering the full Foreign section classification with examples of all categories.

As stated above, almost any available foreign species can be exhibited, although in general terms, some species do better at shows than others. Green Singing Finches (*Serinus mozambicus*) for example, will be placed above the more drably-attired Grey Singing Finches (*S. leucopygius*), although theoretically both species should have an equal chance of taking the red ticket. The fancier, who does not wish to specialise therefore, should select the species which are to comprise his show team with some degree of care.

SHOW CLASSIFICATION OF FOREIGN SPECIES

Classification of foreign birds at the **National Exhibition of Cage and Aviary Birds** at the time of writing, is as follows:

FOREIGN BIRDS

Singly or in Pairs (Cock and Hen)

THE FOREIGN BIRDS SEEDEATERS

651 Red-eared, Orange-cheeked, Gold-breasted, Sundevall's Waxbills and Red Avadavats
652 Common Cordon Bleus, Common Fire Finches
653 St. Helena, Blue-breasted, Blue-capped, Yellow-bellied and Fawn-breasted Waxbills, Lavender Finches and Green Avadavats
654 Cutthroats, Common Silverbills, Spice Birds, Combassous, Grey Java Sparrows, Song Sparrows and Grey and Green Singing Finches
655 All species African and Asiatic Mannikins (Nuns not Manakins) excluding species listed in other classes
656 Red-headed, Saffron, Red-crested, Pileated and Black-crested Finches (Pigmy Cardinals). White Java Sparrows and Pearl-headed Silverbills
657 All species of Whydahs (except common Combassous)
658 All species of Weavers
659 All species of Buntings, Cardinals and Grosbeaks
660 All Gouldian Finches (including colour mutations) and Parrot Finches (including Pin-tailed Nonpareil)
661 Long-tailed 'Heck's' Parsons and Masked Grassfinches
662 All other Australian Seedeaters (Stars, Bichenos, Cherry Finches, Diamond Sparrows etc.)
663 Violet-eared, Grenadier, Black-cheeked and Dufresne's Waxbills, Black-tailed Lavender Finches, all species of Twinspots, all other species of Waxbills and Finches and other seedeating birds not previously listed whose body size is that of a Java Sparrow or less
664 All species of seedeaters not previously listed whose body size is larger than a Java Sparrow
665 Any current-year bred seed-eating bird (bred by exhibitor) listed in classes 651 to 655
666 Any current-year bred seed-eating bird (bred by exhibitor) listed in classes 656 to 664

SOFTBILLS

667 All species of Sunbirds
668 All species of Humming Birds
669 All species of Tanagers (up to and including body size of Flame-faced and Golden-eared)
670 All species of Tanagers larger body size than Flame-faced and Golden-eared (including Scarlet, Sayacca, Silverblue, Mountain etc.)
671 All species of Sugar-birds, Spider Hunters, Flower-peckers, Flower-piercers and Honey-eaters
672 All species of Zosterops
673 Pekin Robins and all species of Fruitsuckers and Bulbuls

674 All species of Robins (except Pekin), Chats, Flycatchers (Niltavas, Minivets etc.), Sibias, Sivas, Mesias, Shamas and Redstarts
675 All species of Mynahs, Starlings, Thrushes, Ground Thrushes, Jay Thrushes, Hangnests and Troupials
676 All species of Birds-of-Paradise, Bower Birds, Cock-of-the-Rock
677 All species of Toucans, Touracos, Toucanettes, Aracaris, Pies and Jays
678 Quails, Doves and Pigeons, any Foreign species
679 All other species of Insect, Fruit and Nectar-feeding birds not previously listed, not larger (body size) than a Pekin Robin
680 All other species of Insect, Fruit and Nectar-feeding birds not previously listed, larger (body size) than a Pekin Robin
681 Any current-year bred Softbill (bred by exhibitor)
682 All Foreign bird Hybrids, Seedeaters and Softbills (one or both parents) and all abnormally coloured Foreign birds and Mutations (not previously listed) including Lutino and Albino (but excluding Parrotlike)

PARROT-LIKE

683 All species of Short-tailed and typical Parrots (Amazons, African Greys etc.)
684 All Cockatoos and Macaws
685 All species normal Lovebirds
686 All Lovebirds mutations and Hybrids
687 Parrotlets, Lineolated Parrakeets and Brotogeris Parrakeets (Tui, Tovi, Canary-winged, Orange-flanked etc.)
688 All species of Hanging Parrots
689 All species of Lories and Lorikeets
690 Normal Cockatiels and normal Red-rump Parrakeets
691 All mutations and abnormally coloured Cockatiels
692 All species of Grass Parrakeets (Bourke's, Turquoisines, Splendids, Elegants etc.)
693 All other Australian and New Zealand Parrakeets
694 Conures (excluding those eligible in Class 687), Quaker, Ringneck and all other long-tailed Parrakeets
695 All mutations and abnormally coloured Parrot-like Birds (except Cockatiels and Lovebirds) Also Hybrids

CURRENT YEAR BRED CLASSES

696 All Lovebirds, Parrotlets and South American Parrakeets (bred by exhibitor)
697 All Australian, Indian, African and Longtailed Parrakeets (bred by exhibitor)
698 All other Parrotlike birds (bred by exhibitor)

This classification is not, unfortunately, standardised, and it generally varies from show to show, with the Foreign Bird enthusiasts on the show-promoting committee frequently influencing the bias towards any particular group. The classification usually followed at the lesser shows is:

1. **Parrot-like** — 2 to 3 Classes
2. **Common Seedeaters** — 3 to 4 Classes
3. **Rare Seedeaters** — 5 to 6 Classes
4. **Softbills** — 6 to 8 Classes

In addition, there has been a very welcome trend in recent years to provide two or three classes in the show schedule for **current-year birds** bred by the exhibitor. Beginners may be confused by the distinction between Common and Rare Seedeaters, and as the classification at most shows is rather anomalous in this respect, the subject is discussed at greater length elsewhere.

PARROT-LIKE BIRDS

The classes for Parrot-like usually comprise one for Lovebirds, Parrotlets and the *Brotogeris* group of smaller Parrakeets, another for the larger Indian and Australian species and, frequently, a third for the typical Short-tailed Parrots and Cockatoos. Occasionally, a fourth class may be included, to provide separate cover for the nectar-feeding Lories, Lorikeets and Hanging Parrots.

It seems inadvisable for the non-specialist fancier to attempt to keep the whole range of Parrot-like species, as many require fairly demanding attention if they are to be properly managed. It is assumed of course in these notes, that the intending exhibitor will be fully aware that, whichever species he selects for his team, the birds must be steady and trained for the show cage before being entered for exhibition.

The suggestion then is, for the Parrot-like section, a pair of Lovebirds — the Black-masked always look striking in perfect feather, a pair of the smaller Australian Grass Parrakeets, such as the Turquoisines or Bourkes, and a pair of Indian Plumhead Parrakeets — which also tend to be in immaculate feather if given half a chance. If the fancier is fortunate enough to own a pet Amazon Parrot or Cockatoo, this will also make an admirable exhibit when in perfect condition.

Other Parrot-like species which frequently do well on the show bench, and which may readily be catered for by the novice, include the South American Quaker Parrakeet, Canary-winged Parrakeet, Meyer's Parrot and the *Pyrrhura* Conures.

The award for *Best Parrot-like* in section is, of course, frequently annexed by fine examples of some of the Australian Broad-tailed Parrakeets, or some of the nectar-feeding Lories and Lorikeets. However, it is suggested here that the latter species are more suitable for the experienced fancier, and the Broadtails never really look very happy in a show cage. Relatively few Parrot-like specialists, in fact, exhibit their stock, deriving their enjoyment in the breeding field rather than in terms of showing, and it must be admitted that it is inadvisable, in the case of species which require fairly spacious accommodation, such as the Rosellas and larger Broadtails, to subject them to the stresses of being confined within the restricted limits of a show cage, for even a few days. Individual birds which are exceptionally tame and steady, of course, may tolerate exhibition conditions quite well.

COMMON SEEDEATERS

The next species to be dealt with, following the classification system generally used by the lesser shows, are the Common Seedeaters. These birds attract most interest initially from novice exhibitors. Each class in this category will normally specify by name the species which may be shown in that class, and this will vary slightly from show to show, being influenced largely by the personal preferences of the organising committee.

Classification for Common Seedeaters

A typical classification for Common Seedeaters at the average open show could be as follows:

1. **Class A — Red-eared and Orange-cheeked Waxbills, Red Avadavats, Common Silverbills, Grey and Green Singing Finches, Sundevall's Waxbills.**
2. **Class B — Common Firefinches, Cordon Bleus, Gold-Breasted Waxbills, St. Helena Waxbills, Yellow-bellied Waxbills.**
3. **Class C — Cutthroats, Grey Java Sparrows, Red-headed Finches, Saffron Finches, all African and Indian Mannikins.**
4. **Class D — Lavender Finches, Green Avadavats, Blue-breasted and Blue-capped Waxbills, Pearl-headed Silverbills, Cuban and Olive Finches.**

Although the above classes are typical of those provided for *Common* Seedeaters at the majority of shows, it will immediately be apparent, even to fairly inexperienced fanciers, that a few of the

1
2

species covered by this classification can, by no means, be regarded as 'common'. The term 'common' in the context of exhibiting foreign species, of course, indicates that the species in question is freely (and cheaply) available, on a regular basis, to fanciers in this country, rather than that it is plentiful in its country of origin. In the above-mentioned classification, however, are included the Cuban Finch (*Tiaris canora*) and the Olive Finch (*Tiaris olivacea*), neither of which can be regarded as having been freely available in recent years. Furthermore, the grouping of *all* African and Indian Mannikins in one class would encompass the scarcer species as well as the common. It could also be reasonably argued that the Red-headed Finch (*Amadina erythrocephala*) is far less common than the closely-related Cut-throat (*A. fasciata*) although both are generally included in the same class.

It would, however, be almost impossible for any organisation promoting shows to devise a realistic classification which would cater for all potentially available foreign species, without creating some anomalies. The fancier must, therefore, learn to accept that the award for **Best Common Seedeater** may occasionally be won by a species which is not freely available, and as a corollary, of course, the **Rare Seedeater award** may sometimes go to a fairly common species.

Class A

Red-eared and Orange-cheeked Waxbills, Red Avadavats, Common Silverbills, Grey and Green Singing Finches, Sundevall's Waxbills.

With regard to selecting suitable species to form a show team in

---

◄

1.1 **Black-Cheeked Lovebirds and a Black-Winged Lory**

1. **Black-Cheeked Lovebirds** (*Agapornis nigrigenis*) Length 6 inches (15 cm)
An East African species less common in Britain than some of the other Lovebird Species, but bred regularly in small numbers. The facial area is not, in fact, black but a very deep, dark brown, which contrasts nicely with the remainder of the grass-green plumage. Lovebirds are ideal subjects for the novice exhibitor, being hardy and fairly easy to maintain in good feather. Some species are also quite easy to breed and the number of colour mutations has proliferated in the past few years.
2. **Black-Winged Lory** (*Eos cyanogenia*)
A number of different species of Lories are regularly imported each year; this is one of the rarer examples. Found on the islands in Geelvink Bay, New Guinea, it frequents the coconut palms near the coast. The brush-tongued Lories and Lorikeets require a diet of varied fruits and suitable nectar paste, which tends to dissuade some fanciers from keeping them. Once acclimatised, however, they are hardy and extremely beautiful, their principal drawbacks being the messy nature of their copious liquid droppings and their often unpleasantly loud voices.

the Common Seedeater section, let us first consider Class A. Virtually any of the species mentioned by name in this class would be capable of doing well, with the possible exception of the Grey Singing Finch, whose marvellous singing ability is not, unfortunately, an attribute on the show bench. Included in this class are the least expensive of all foreign species, many thousands of which are imported into Europe every year, and because of this relative abundance it is essential that only the most outstanding are selected for exhibition purposes.

There is a considerable variation in size among individuals of the various Waxbill species, for example; and, although I have expressed the view that size alone should not be regarded as the criterion of a bird's perfection, it is necessary to select individuals of good substance if they are to attract the attention of the judge.

One species in this class, which has always done well for myself, and other exhibitors, is the Green Singing Finch. Its brightly-coloured plumage and fine feather texture, coupled with its bold, alert demeanour generally ensure it a place 'in the cards' if staged in faultless condition. It is wise therefore, to endeavour to include a pair of Green Singers in the show team, with probably a good pair of Red-eared or Orange-cheeked Waxbills as a back-up entry.

Class B

Common Firefinches, Cordon Bleus, Gold-breasted Waxbills, St. Helena Waxbills, Yellow-bellied Waxbills.

Class B may be regarded as wide open, in the sense that any of the species included would be capable of carrying off the honours if correctly staged. However, my particular favourite in this group is the Firefinch, one of the most delightful of the whole Waxbill family, and quite capable of taking the award for **Best Common Seedeater**. Perfection of feathering is an important show requisite of this species, particularly in the case of the male, as even a single missing feather will create quite a noticeable blemish on the otherwise smooth, evenly-coloured surface of the plumage. Female Firefinches are notoriously delicate and there is generally a surplus

1.2 **Vinaceous Firefinch** (*Lagonosticta vinacea*)
One of the delightful family of African Firefinches, the Vinaceous is not as frequently imported as the Common or Red-billed species. Females are especially delicate and require careful acclimatisation. When available, this West African species is an ideal exhibit for the Rare Seedeater classes.

of males among dealers' stocks; if it is found impossible to acquire a suitable female, it is quite permissible to exhibit a single male without a partner and, if the bird is of suitable quality and condition, he is quite capable of winning the class or sub-section.

These remarks could apply equally well to the Cordon Bleu, of course, and my reason for selecting the Firefinch is simply a matter of personal preference. Perhaps it should be added at this point that the term 'Common Firefinches' used in the context of this class refers to the species known variously as the Firefinch, the Common Firefinch, the Senegal Firefinch or the Red-billed Firefinch (*Lagonosticta senegala*). It also includes the East African race (the so-called "Giant Firefinch"), but not other distinct species such as Jameson's Firefinch, and others.

Class C

Cut-throats, Grey Java Sparrows, Red-headed Finches, Saffron Finches, all African and Indian Mannikins.

If we now turn our attention to Class C, we find a group of species of differing characteristics. Probably one of the most popular species in this class is the Grey Java Sparrow. The simple colour scheme of this Indonesian bird is quite striking and the beautifully-textured plumage is almost invariably in immaculate condition. However, because judges are aware that the species is relatively easy to maintain in such condition, the Java Sparrow is frequently passed over in favour of the less-common species which share the same class.

Although, as it has already been pointed out, the Red-headed

1.3 **Mannikins**

1. **Tri-coloured Mannikin** (*Lonchura malacca malacca*) Length 4½ inches (11.4 cm)
Imported from India in considerable numbers each year this species has always been popular with beginners. Quietly but attractively garbed in chocolate, white and black, the Tri-coloured Mannikin is hardy and easy to manage.
2. **Black-Headed Mannikin** (*Lonchura malacca antricapilla*) Length 4½ inches (11.4 cm)
Another commonly-imported member of the munia family, it is, like most of the Asiatic Mannikins, easy to cater for and hardy when properly acclimatised. One problem with this, and similar species, is the tendency for their claws to become overgrown in confinement. The claws should be regularly inspected and trimmed carefully as necessary.
3. **White-Headed Mannikin** (*Lonchura maja*) Length 4½ inches (11.4 cm)
A native of Sumatra, Java and Malaya the White-headed Mannikin is rather less frequently available than the two preceding species. It is however just as suitable for the inexperienced fancier and can generally prove a useful exhibit in the Common Seedeater classes if immaculately staged.

MANNIKINS.

(1) *Tri-coloured.* (2) *Black-headed.* (3) *White-headed.*

Finch (*Amadina erythrocephala*) is only occasionally available to aviculturists in this country, it is worthwhile expending some effort in trying to acquire a pair. It is a bold-looking species of pleasing colouring and is likely to catch the judge's eye when shown among the commoner species with which it generally has to compete.

The smaller Cut-throat or Ribbon Finch (*Amadina fasciata*) is one of the African species which has been regularly imported into Europe in large numbers during much of the twentieth century. There is considerable variation in the density and shade of the plumage pattern, due partly to geographical race divergence, and it is essential to select male and female of identical shade and distribution of markings. In spite of the fact that this is such an extremely common species, the merits of a perfectly-matched pair of Cut-throats staged in faultless condition will be recognised by a competent judge.

Normally, also included in this class are all the African and Indian Mannikins. Under this broad heading we find such species as the Bronze-winged Mannikin (*Spermestes cucullatus*), Rufous-backed Mannikin (*S. nigriceps*), Tricoloured Nun (*Lonchura malacca*) and Black-headed Mannikin (*L. atricapilla*).

If the classification is to be strictly observed, the White-headed Mannikin (*L. maja*) however, would not be eligible for inclusion in this class, as this species is found in Java and other islands of Indonesia. Similarly, other island species should not be entered in this class.

As can be seen from the foregoing, the exhibitor may select from a fairly wide range of species when deciding on his entries in this class. The entry suggested here is a pair of Red-headed Finches, if obtainable, or alternatively a *good* pair of Cut-throats or Rufous-backed Mannikins.

Class D

Lavender Finches, Green Avadavats, Blue-breasted and Blue-capped Waxbills, Pearl-headed Silverbills, Cuban and Olive Finches.

The last of the typical classes in the Common Seedeater grouping includes those species which may be regarded as slightly less common than most of the seedeaters which have been mentioned previously without actually falling into the category of *rare*. The anomaly of the Cuban and Olive Finches has already been discussed.

A personal preference in this class, of the species which are fairly readily available, would be a pair of Lavender Finches with, additionally or alternatively, a pair of Pearl-headed Silverbills. The former species is rather prone to feather-plucking in confinement, and Lavender Finches should never, therefore, be housed in overcrowded or very restricted accommodation. A steady pair of Lavender Finches staged in perfect condition is extremely attractive and, as most judges are well aware of the problems of achieving perfect plumage with this species, they can hold their own in any competition. Species other than those listed are sometimes included in this class, particularly Black-crested Finches (the so-called Pigmy Cardinal), Red-crested Finches and Quail Finches. Even in those instances where these additional species are defined in the classification, the two species already mentioned are still recommended.

CHAPTER 2

Show Species II
Rare Seedeaters and Softbills

In the preceding chapter the classification generally followed for foreign birds is shown to be as follows:

1. **Parrot-like**
2. **Common Seedeaters**
3. **Rare Seedcaters**
4. **Softbills**

In that chapter, the Parrot-like birds and Common Seedeaters are discussed. This chapter is concerned with the Rare Seedeaters and Softbills.

RARE SEEDEATERS

The classes for the Rare Seedeaters are also variable in content, and are subject to similar anomalies as those discussed with regard to Parrot-like birds and Common Seedeaters, in that they encompass a considerable number of species which are relatively common in avicultural terms.

Classification

The following classification is a typical average based on a selection of open shows and covers practically all the species or groups of species likely to be encountered:

1. **Class E — All species of Australian Seedeaters and Parrot Finches.**
2. **Class F — Grenadier Waxbills, Violet-eared Waxbills, Melba Finches, all Pytilias and Twinspots.**
3. **Class G — All species of Whydahs and Typical Weavers.**
4. **Class H — All species of Buntings, Cardinals, Grosbeaks, Doves, Quail, White Java Sparrows and all other species of seedeaters not previously mentioned, whose body size is that of a Java Sparrow or larger, including hybrids and colour mutations.**
5. **Class J — All other species of seedeaters not previously mentioned, whose body size is less than that of a Java Sparrow.**

2.1 **Red-Headed Parrot-Finches** (*Erythrura psittacea*) Length 5½ inches (14 cm)
A handsome, brightly-coloured species from New Guinea, with red face and grass-green body plumage. Aviary-bred specimens are fairly frequently available but in very limited numbers and command quite high prices. They are lively and active birds and require to be reasonably steady in the show cage if they are to have a chance of success in stiff competition.

Class E

Australian Seedeaters and Parrot Finches.

Since the inauguration of the **Australian Finch Society** in 1971, interest in keeping Australian seedeaters has flourished greatly, with the greatest progress being made in the field of breeding rather than exhibiting. However, the numbers and variety of Australian species being exhibited have increased considerably since the Society was formed and some show-promoting societies have extended the number of classes for Australian seedeaters to two. In such cases Class E has usually been sub-divided to provide one class for the *Poephila* Grassfinches (Heck's, Parson Finches, etc.) together with species such as the Diamond Firetail, Star Finch,

2.2 **Bicheno's Finches** (*Stizoptera bichenovii*) Length 4 inches (10 cm)
Named after J.E. Bicheno, secretary of the Linnean Society in London (1825-1832), this species is another of the very popular Australian grassfinches. Regularly available, albeit in fairly limited numbers, it is difficult to sex which possibly accounts for at least some of its breeding failures. It is delicately marked in various shades of brown, black and white, and can be a most useful addition to the show team.

Chestnut-breasted Finch, Cherry Finch and Bicheno's Finch. The other class caters for the Gouldian Finches and Parrot Finches.

Since the Australian Government imposed a total ban on the export of the native fauna of that country in the 1960's, the only Australian avian species available to aviculturists have been those bred in confinement. Although considerable numbers of Australian seedeaters are now bred annually in this country, there are also substantial numbers of such birds being imported from the Continent (Holland and Belgium), as well as from Japan and the Far East. Lesser numbers have also originated from other sources, including South Africa, as in the case of the beautiful White-breasted mutation of the Gouldian Finch.

Because of these large numbers, all of which are produced in confinement, there is inevitably a wide variation in the quality of individual birds, particularly those which are most prolific. It seems, therefore, even more important than usual, to pay particular attention to the quality of the stock rather than the species when selecting exhibits for this class.

Virtually all the available Australian seedeaters have an equal chance of winning their class, with the possible exception of the Star Finch, which generally appears to be passed over, except in the case of really outstanding specimens before a very knowledgeable judge. The Gouldian Finch, in its various colour forms, is quite popular with exhibitors and, unfortunately, there is a tendency for some judges to allocate red tickets to representatives of this species, irrespective of the quality of the birds. It appears that such judges are basing their decisions on the fact that the Gouldian was, in the not too distant past, considered to be a fairly scarce and delicate species, and that the judges have not had sufficient experience with these birds to differentiate between good and bad specimens.

Apart from other considerations, special attention should be paid to the length of the elongated median feathers in the tails of Gouldians, Long-tailed and Heck's Grassfinches, as this characteristic is very variable. The Heck's Grassfinch is a geographical sub-species of the Long-tailed species, differing only in the colour of the bill, which is sealing-wax red in the case of the former and yellow in the latter. Unfortunately, much interbreeding between the two races has been allowed to take place, with the result that the bill colour of the Heck's Grassfinch, which is genetically dominant, has been reduced to orange in many cases. Lack of the true deep colour in the bills of the Heck's sub-species would, in my view, constitute a show fault.

There is, in fact, one species in this class which is generally available only as wild-caught individuals. The Pintailed Nonpareil (*Erythrura prasina*) is a Parrot Finch originating from Indonesia and is not, therefore, subject to the extremely stringent export restrictions which govern the availability of the Australasian species. It makes a useful exhibit if staged in steady condition.

Class F

Grenadier Waxbills, Violet-eared Waxbills, Melba finches, all Pytilias and Twinspots

The next class is that for the rarer Estrildines and is probably the most fairly balanced of all the seedeater classes. All the species

2.3 **Violet-Eared Waxbills** (*Uraeginthus granatinus*) Length 5½ inches (14 cm)
Fairly common in the wild, in the northern part of Southern Africa, the Violet-eared has never been imported in large numbers, although it is offered by dealers quite regularly. A strikingly handsome Waxbill with its unusual plumage colouring of violet and rich chocolate brown, it is a superb exhibit for the Rare Seedeater classes, but is more suitable for the experienced aviculturist.

eligible for entry in this class are virtually equal in size, rarity and delicacy, and all are strikingly beautiful. None can be regarded as 'easy' species for the beginner and careful management is required, particularly during the immediate post-importation and acclimatisation period.

The novice who wishes to exhibit in this class, and who also has sufficient time and dedication to devote to the welfare of his birds, could consider acquiring a suitably acclimatised pair of Melba Finches or Crimson-winged Pytilias (Aurora Finches). It would certainly be advisable for the fancier to gain as much experience and knowledge as possible with some of the hardier species before undertaking the care of those which are more delicate.

2.4 **Melba Finch** (*Pytelia melba*)
An attractive species from Southern Africa, it requires careful acclimatisation when first imported.

Class G

Whydahs and Typical Weavers

This is a fascinating range of African and Asiatic species; most of the males are colourful in their striking breeding plumage, some are polygamous and some are brood parasitic. It seems certain that it is only the fact that virtually all the species are difficult to breed in confinement, which limits the popularity of this group with aviculturists.

As this class generally covers *all* species of Whydahs and Typical Weavers, we again have a situation where fairly common species will be competing against their rarer relatives. The problems of eclipse plumage are discussed in Chapter 5, and because of the uncertainty which arises with these species in this respect, if accommodation permits, it would be useful to possess, say, two pairs of Whydahs and a pair of Weavers. For some reason, the latter species do not appear to be very popular with foreign bird judges and it is only on very rare occasions that any species of

Weaver progresses beyond class winner to reach the **Best Rare Seedeater** position. Whydahs, on the other hand, do take such awards more frequently, although, of course, more care is necessary in order to stage the males in perfect condition, on account of the elongated tail feathers.

Whydahs

The most commonly-available Whydahs are the Paradise (*Steganura paradisea*) and the Pintailed (*Vidua macroura*), either of which makes a useful exhibit for the novice. However, it is suggested here a pair of Fischer's Whydahs (*V. fischeri*) be obtained when circumstances permit. Less frequently imported than the two preceding species, the Fischer's is occasionally offered for sale and generally gives a good account of itself in this class, if carefully staged.

The shorter-tailed Whydahs tend to be more restless and require much time and patience to acquire the desired degree of steadiness. They appear to fare badly in competition with their long-tailed relatives at the majority of the shows, and appear to be by-passed by all but the most specialist of judges. One of this group of Whydahs, which I kept for a number of years was a male Red-naped (*Coliuspasser ardens laticauda*), which is the North-East African sub-species of the Red-collared Whydah (*C. ardens ardens*). Although the bird's success on the show bench before a variety of judges was, on the whole, mediocre, he was found to be far less aggressive towards other, and smaller companions than some of the species mentioned above.

As an additional entry for this class a keen fancier might try to obtain one of the rarer species, which very occasionally appear on the market, such as the Queen Whydah (*V.regia*), Giant Whydah (*Coliuspasser progne*) or Jackson's Whydah (*Drepanoplectes jacksoni*). These rarer species, when once obtained, are not difficult to keep in good health, but great care is necessary if their fine plumage is to be kept immaculate throughout the show season.

Weavers

The choice of Weaver species available to the aviculturist is, if anything, more extensive than in the case of the Whydahs. By far the commonest is the Red-billed Weaver (or Quelea), an African species which has been described as one of the most numerous birds in the world. It is true that gigantic flocks of these birds have presented an economic threat to agricultural crops to such an extent, that it was reported a few years ago that napalm bombing was being employed against vast colonies in South Africa in an effort to control their numbers.

Almost all the Weavers, and particularly the Red-billed, are of a restless disposition and it generally requires a considerable amount of time and patience to produce a suitable state of steadiness in a show cage. Although the Red-billed Weaver is rather an attractive species, in a modest sort of way when in breeding plumage, it is not too successful as an exhibition species.

This is due partly to its abundance and partly to the failure of many exhibitors to bench it in a suitably steady condition. A further point to watch, if one proposes showing this species, is the possibility of confusing the Red-billed Weaver with its dimorphic form known as Russ's Weaver. The male Red-billed species in breeding plumage possesses a black face-mask which is absent in the female, and, in the dimorphic male this mask is replaced by one of a pink-fawn hue. On occasions, male Russ's Weavers can be seen being exhibited as partners to male Red-billed Weavers in the mistaken belief that they were females of the latter species.

There are many species of Weaver from which to select one's show specimens, although some are imported only irregularly. Many of the 'Yellow' Weavers (*Ploceus* spp.) are rather similar in colour and pattern of plumage, and may not be readily identified by all judges. It is preferable to obtain one of the less commonly imported and distinctive species such as the Chestnut Weaver (*Ploceus rubiginosus*) or the scarcer Thick-billed Weaver (*Amblyospiza albifrons*), particularly as the winner of this class will be required to compete for the Rare Seedeater award and not that for Common Seedeaters.

Class H

All species of Buntings, Cardinals, Grosbeaks, Doves, Quail, White Java Sparrows and all other species of seedeaters not previously mentioned, whose body size is that of a Java Sparrow or larger, including hybrids and colour mutations.

The governing feature of this class is size, but there is one exception, the Buntings, which are included in this class but which are, in some instances, smaller than the Java Sparrow. The class may contain a real mixed bag with species ranging from the exquisite South American Rainbow Bunting (*Passerina leclancheri*) to some of

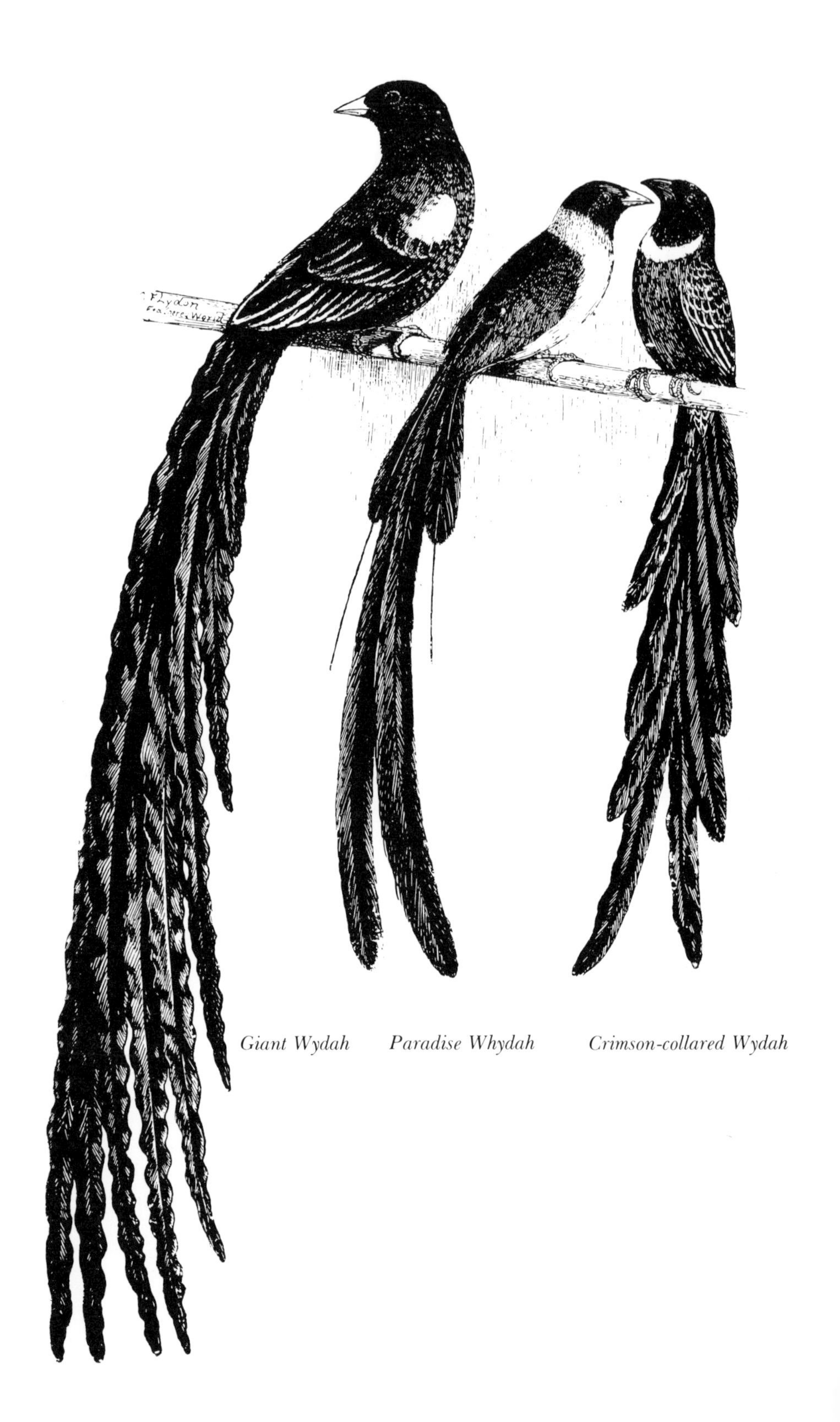

Giant Wydah *Paradise Whydah* *Crimson-collared Wydah*

the larger members of the Dove family (*Columbidae*).

The exhibits which are usually to be found in this class at the average open show tend to be the White Java Sparrow, Diamond and Namaqua Doves, Quail of various species, and the occasional Cardinal. A first class pair of White Java Sparrows will often do well in this sort of competition, but they must be really good, with not the slightest suspicion of grey flecking. A well-staged pair of one of the *Dove* species will also give a good account of themselves, particularly as most judges appreciate that these birds are rather soft-feathered and are consequently not the easiest of species to stage in faultless condition. However, as the classification allows the exhibitor a wide range of choice in this instance, the acquisition of one of the lesser-known exotics might pay dividends where the competition is strong. One of the **Asiatic Hawfinches**, for example, can make a striking exhibit and the Black-headed species (*Eophona personata*) is occasionally available in this country. Practically all the South American Buntings (*Passerina* spp.) are of eye-catching appearance and worthy of consideration for a place in the show team, being generally preferable to the Cardinals and Grosbeaks.

Class J

All other species of seedeaters not previously mentioned, whose body size is less than that of a Java Sparrow.

The exhibits eligible for this class at any given show will, of course, depend on the specification of the previous classes, but

---

2.5 **Whydahs**

1. Giant Whydah (*Coliuspasser progne*)
   Length 22 inches (56 cm) Male in full breeding plumage.
   A magnificent species from Central and Southern Africa which is only rarely available to aviculturists in this country. The Giant Whydah has, however, been bred in Britain. The Whydahs are very hardy on the whole and are suitable for novice exhibitors although the long tail plumes must be maintained in perfect condition.
2. Paradise Whydah (*Steganura paradisea*)
   Length 15 inches (38 cm) Male in full breeding plumage.
   One of the most frequently available Whydahs, this Central African species is popular with exhibitors. It is believed to be polygamous and is certainly brood-parasitic, laying its eggs primarily in the nests of Melba Finches (*Pytelia melba*).
3. Red-Collared Whydah (*Coliuspasser ardens ardens*)
   Length 14 inches (35.5 cm) Male in full breeding plumage.
   A native of Southern Africa, this Whydah is quite a useful exhibit when in full colour. It is more striking in appearance than its sub-species, the Red-naped Whydah (*C.a. laticauda*) which is found in Abyssinia and North-east Africa.

2.6 **Black-Headed Siskin** (*Spinus ictericus*)
Length 5 inches (13 cm)
The most commonly-imported of the South American Siskins, its plumage is a pleasant combination of greens, yellows and black. The Black-headed Siskin should not be confused with the Hooded Siskin (*S. cucullatus*) which is one of the genetic forebears of the Red Factor Canary. As an exhibition species, the Black-headed's success has been generally unspectacular.

generally they will consist of some of the rarer Waxbills, Serins, South American Finches (*Sporophila* spp.) and a number of other assorted species.

During one of those influxes of rarely-available species, which occur from time to time, Black-capped and Fawn-breasted Waxbills recently appeared in dealers' advertisements in this country for a short time. Either of these delightful species would constitute an excellent exhibit for the class under consideration, although normally they are virtually unobtainable. Alternatively, one of the South American species, such as the Lined Finch (*Sporophila americana*), Jacarini Finch (*Volatinia jacarini*) or Black-headed Siskin (*Spinus ictericus*), would prove to be a suitable entry, and any of these should be available fairly regularly.

2.7 **Parson Finch x Bengalese Hybrid** (*Poephila cincta x Lonchura striata dom.*)
Length 4¾ inches (12 cm)
A considerable number of Bengalese hybrids are bred each year — mostly resulting from matings with other munias. From the exhibition point of view, hybrids should clearly show the characteristics of both parents, but as a rule their fortunes on the show bench are rather mixed. Even in the absence of show *standards* it is difficult to relate the quality of a bird of hybrid parentage to that of pure-bred species. Many (but not all) hybrids prove to be infertile when mated to each other or back to one of the parents.

Hybrids

In this class, and in the previous one, are also included Hybrids and colour mutations of the appropriate body sizes. Many foreign bird hybrids are produced by chance rather than design, with interbreeding between different species usually taking place where odd birds of different sexes are housed in communal aviaries. Generally, hybridisation occurs between fairly closely-related species and is probably most prevalent among Munias, with such crosses as Bengalese × Spice Bird, Silverbill × Spice Bird, among others, being fairly common on the show bench. Less common hybrids can be seen on exhibition, of course, including Diamond Firetail × Zebra Finch, Bengalese × Diamond Firetail. Although they have a certain curiosity value, it seems that the production of hybrids is a rather pointless exercise unless one is undertaking serious research into the evolutionary development of the species involved.

Hybrids do appear occasionally, however, by accident and the owner may wish to exhibit them in the appropriate class. In addition to the normal criteria used in assessing the exhibition qualities of true species, the most important feature of any hybrid is that it should clearly possess the characteristics of both parent species. In other words, its parentage should be readily identifiable by its physical appearance — a requirement which is not possessed by all hybrids.

SOFTBILLS

Of all the sub-divisions of the Foreign Bird classification, the one for Softbills undoubtedly shows the widest divergence, with some show schedules having as few as two classes and others as many as eleven. This variation is perhaps understandable when the reader considers the great variety of Softbill species which are potentially available to the exhibitor and the relative paucity of the actual numbers imported at any one time.

At those open shows, where a fairly good entry of foreign species may be anticipated, it is advantageous to provide a comprehensive classification, as this will tend to encourage exhibitors to enter more exhibits than would be the case if only two or three classes were included. In order to cater for most of the available Softbill species in a manner which is as fair and just as possible, it will generally be necessary to provide a minimum of nine classes in this grouping.

Classification

The suggested classification, which is detailed below, shows a typical layout of the various groups of species, although the actual constitution of each class may vary from show to show:

1. Class K — All species of Humming-birds and Sunbirds.
2. Class L — All species of Tanagers, not larger than the Superb, and all species of Manakins.
3. Class M — All species of Tanagers, larger than the Superb, and all species of Fruitsuckers and Bulbuls.
4. Class N — All species of Zosterops, Yuhinas, Flowerpeckers and Ixulus.
5. Class O — All species of Robins, Chats, Flycatchers and Redstarts.
6. Class P — All species of Sibias, Sivas, Mesias, Shamas, Dhyal Birds and Pekin Robins.
7. Class Q — All species of Mynahs, Thrushes, Starlings, Hangnests and Troupials.
8. Class R — All other species of Softbills and Nectar Feeders not larger in body size than a Pekin Robin.
9. Class S — All other species of Softbills and Nectar Feeders larger in body size than a Pekin Robin.

Class K

Nectar-feeders — the Humming birds (*Trochilidae*) **and the Sunbirds** (*Nectariniidae*).

Occasionally it will be found that the South American Sugarbirds (*Dacnidinae*) are also included in this class but they are more often catered for in the following one along with the Smaller Tanagers. None of these species are particularly suitable for the novice exhibitor and all impose considerable demands in terms of time and knowledge of their requirements. Of the two families, that from the Old World — the Sunbirds — is generally regarded as being the least difficult to cater for. The Humming birds, of which there are some 319 species, are quite expensive to purchase, very difficult to breed, generally aggressive and are, on the whole, suitable for only the most experienced of aviculturists. The Sunbirds, on the other hand, can prove to be quite hardy when properly acclimatised and usually prove successful on the show bench when staged in good order. It is necessary to remember, of course, that however rare or wonderful the species, it can only win if exhibited in perfect condition, and even the rarest Humming bird should never be given precedence over a Common Silverbill unless it is superior in both condition and quality.

The Sunbirds are the Old World equivalents of the American Humming birds and their many species are distributed over a wide geographical range. Although these beautiful avian gems — excuse the cliche but it is really most apt — are now much less freely available than they were a few years ago, both in quantity and variety, a few appear regularly on the market and are firm favourites with the experienced exhibitor.

In view of the tremendous number of species which would be eligible for entry in this class when available, it is rather difficult to suggest any one which would be more suitable than the rest. However my particular favourites, which are also among the most beautiful of the Sunbirds, include the Marico Sunbird (*Nectarinia mariquensis*), Malachite Sunbird (*N. famosa*) and the Purple Sunbird (*N. asiatica*). The first two species are to be found in Southern Africa, while the last-named, as its trivial name implies, is to be found in India and South East Asia. It should be added, incidentally, that many species of Sunbirds don their brightly-coloured plumage during the breeding season only, in a similar manner to the Weavers and Whydahs. As this can add to the exhibitor's problems during the show season it may be prudent to select a species which has no eclipse plumage phase, such as the Marico Sunbird.

Class L

All species of Tanagers, not larger than the Superb and the Manakins

The Manakins must not be confused with the similarly-named Mannikins which are, of course, the Asiatic and African seed-eating Munias of the *Ploceidae* family. The Manakins are a relatively small family (*Pipridae*) of some sixty South American insectivorous species which occur from southern Mexico to Argentina. Very few of the Manakins are available in this country but the Blue-backed species (*Chiroxiphia pareola*) is occasionally offered by dealers, and makes a delightful exhibit. They are small birds, some 3½ inches (9 cm) in length.

The other contestants in this class also originate from the New World. The Tanagers (*Thraupidae*) are a family of some 220 species, most of which are confined to the South American countries. They are, in the main, brilliantly-coloured and have a liking for soft fruits which necessitates extra care in ensuring that their environment and plumage are kept scrupulously clean. The smaller Tanagers are those up to about the size of the Superb species (*Tangara fastuosa*) which is about 5½ inches (14 cm) in length. Again because of the number of species, it is difficult to decide which may be regarded as the most suitable for a show team, but those which are likely to catch the judge's eye would include, in addition to the

Superb, the Emerald-spotted (*T. chrysophrys*), Mrs. Wilson's (*T. nigrocincta franciscae*) and the Violet (*T. violacea*).

Class M

All species of Tanagers larger than the Superb, the Fruitsuckers and Bulbuls.

The Fruitsuckers (*Chloropseidae*) are a small family of Asiatic species, mainly green in colour, and are also known as Leafbirds. The Bulbul family (*Pycnonotidae*) on the other hand comprises some 120 species distributed throughout Asia and Africa.

The Silver-Blue (*Thraupis virens*) is one of the most beautiful of the larger Tanagers although it is by no means the rarest, and lacks the gaudy plumage of some of the other species. Its attractive pastel colouring and fine texture of feather, however, ensure that it will not pass unnoticed. As an alternative one might consider the bold and striking Blue-winged Mountain Tanager as a representative of the larger species.

Although the Golden-fronted Fruitsucker (*Chloropsis aurifrons*) is the most commonly imported of its family, its close relative the Orange-bellied or Hardwick's species (*C. hardwickii*) is generally the more successful on the show bench when available.

In the case of the Bulbuls, the Asiatic species provide the most frequently available members of the family, namely the Red-vented (*Pycnonotus cafer*), Red-whiskered (*P. jocosus*) and White-eared (*P. leucotis*). Although these three are attractive and ideal exhibits for the novice Softbill exhibitor, they may not prove an equal match for the Hardwick's Fruitsucker or one of the Tanagers mentioned above. It would, therefore, be prudent to try and obtain one of the less common Bulbul species such as the Black-crested (*P. melanicterus*) or Scaly-breasted (*P. squamatus*), if the fancier is particularly interested in this family of birds.

Class N

All species of Zosterops, Yuhinas, Flowerpeckers and Ixulus

In this class there is a nice selection of the more diminutive species, although it may be argued that the class is a little unbalanced in that the Indian Zosterops (*Zosterops palpebrosa*) and others of the *Zosteropidae* family are considerably less rare than the **Flowerpeckers**. The latter are tiny, beautiful birds of which the males are usually brightly-coloured and comprise a total of fifty-

eight species. They are imported irregularly and in very small numbers, but they are occasionally available, and well merit the attention of the experienced fancier who will find them a most charming exhibit. Species which have been imported, and which, incidentally, include the most colourful members of the family, are the Orange-bellied Flowerpecker (*Dicaeum trigonostigma*), the Scarlet-backed (*D. cruentatum*) and the Crimson-breasted (*Prionochilus percussus*).

The Zosterops, of which there are eighty-two species in Africa and Asia, are all of a similar appearance and it is quite difficult to identify many of the species without careful study. One of the most attractive — although none of them are unattractive — is the Chestnut-flanked species (*Z. erythropleura*) and this would be an excellent choice as a member of the show team.

Class O

All species of Robins, Chats, Flycatchers and Redstarts

This class caters for a diverse and, in many cases, beautiful group of species. The choice of exhibits is such that it is difficult to recommend any particular species, as availability will largely control the selection. Undoubtedly one of the most successful groups in this class — in exhibition terms — is that of the **Flycatchers**. In this group alone are to be found some beautiful and striking

2.8 **South American Tanagers**

1. **Magpie Tanager** (*Cissopis leveriana*)
   Length 8½ inches (21.6 cm)
   One of the larger Tanager species, the Magpie is not imported very frequently. It can be rather aggressive towards smaller species and care should be taken therefore in providing suitable accommodation. There are two sub-species: *C.l. leveriana*, which is found in the Upper Amazon region and *C.l. major* whose range extends from Paraguay to South-east Brazil and Northern Argentina. This species frequents the forest edge.
2. **Blue-grey Tanager** (*Thraupis episcopus*)
   Length 6–7 inches (15–18 cm)
   There are 13 sub-species of *T. episcopus* with a wide range over several South American countries. They are all attractive, easy to cater for and hardy when acclimatised.
3. **Silver-blue Tanager** (*Thraupis episcopus virens*)
   Length 6–7 inches (15–18 cm)
   The various sub-species of the Blue-grey Tanager (*T. episcopus*) are of generally similar appearance, differing principally in the colour of the conspicuous patches of blue or white on the wing-coverts. Various popular names are used to describe the more commonly–imported sub-species and trade descriptions may not always be entirely accurate.

2.9 **Blue-Winged Siva** (*Minla cyanouroptera*)
Length 6½ inches (16.5 cm)
Ranges from the Himalayas to South-west China. One of the large family of Babblers (*Timaliidae*) the Siva is frequently imported and makes a useful exhibit for the novice Softbill fancier.

species such as the Tickell's Blue Flycatcher (*Cyornis tickelliae*), Verditer Flycatcher (*Muscicapa thalassina*), Rufous-bellied Niltava (*Niltava sundara*) or, representing the Monarchs, the Asian Paradise Flycatcher (*Terpsiphone paradisi*), which exists in a White phase as well as the Rufous. All of these have taken the award for **Best Foreign Exhibit** at open shows in this country, which must be sufficient recommendation, although many species of Flycatcher are only suitable for the experienced aviculturist.

One species, eligible for this class, which I have always considered to be most beautiful is the River Chat (*Thamnolaea leucocephala*), with its dazzling white crown contrasting with jet black plumage and chestnut tail and underparts. When available it is generally offered by dealers in this country under the name of White-capped Redstart.

2.10 A sleek specimen of the **Purple Glossy Starling** (*Lamprotornis purpureus*).

Class P

All species of Sibias, Sivas, Mesias, Shamas, Dhyal Birds and Pekin Robins

This class includes a number of the more freely-available species and is, on the whole, fairly well-balanced. The Pekin Robin (*Leiothrix lutea*) is probably the most popular of foreign Softbills as far as the novice exhibitor is concerned, and is quite a successful exhibit where the competition is not too strong. In case anyone should be confused as to why the Pekin Robin is not eligible for entry in the previous class (which caters for 'all species of Robins'), it should perhaps be explained that this species is not, in fact a true Robin. The Robins form a sub-division of the Thrush family (*Turdidae*), whereas the Pekin Robin and the closely-related Silver-eared Mesia (*Leiothrix argentauris*) are part of the large family of Babblers (*Timaliidae*). The Shama (*Copsychus malabaricus*) is suggested here as a useful exhibit in this class of competition.

Class Q

All species of Mynahs, Thrushes, Starlings, Hangnests and Troupials

This class allows a very wide range from which to select exhibits, and much will depend on personal preference. Many of the commoner species of Mynahs and Starlings, for example, are very hardy and make ideal subjects for the less experienced exhibitor. One of the most beautiful of the Glossy Starlings to be found in Africa is the Superb Spreo (*Spreo superbus*) and this is a very desirable exhibit for this class. Alternatively, if the fancier's preference lies with the Thrush family, the Chestnut-bellied Rock Thrush (*Monticola rufiventris*) is occasionally available and worthy of consideration. There are, of course, other Thrush and Starling species which make admirable exhibits and it is from one of these two groups that I would tend to select my entry for this class.

Class R

All other species of Softbills and Nectar Feeders not larger in body size than a Pekin Robin

Although the theoretical choice in this class is almost limitless, considering the number of species which exist world-wide, such factors as export restrictions, conservation, political upheaval, transportation, acclimatisation and other difficulties result in only relatively few species being available to aviculturists in this country. Supplies of these 'non-classified' Softbills, therefore, tend to be sporadic and the fancier's choice will be governed, not only by experience, which is the most important criterion, but also by the opportunity to purchase.

The Tits are one of the families which can provide suitable exhibits for the less experienced exhibitor in this class. They are, in fact, divided into three families but it is the *Paridae* which comprises the greatest number of species, some of which are not too difficult to cater for, particularly as some of the Asiatic Tits are geographical races of the European species. Two species which have been imported fairly frequently are the Great Tit (*Parus major*) and the Green-backed Tit (*P. monticolus*).

Other interesting exhibits which can do well in this class are the Nuthatches, of which the Velvet-fronted species (*Sitta frontalis*) is occasionally imported, and the smaller Kingfishers. The African Pygmy Kingfisher (*Ispidina picta*) is probably the best known to Foreign Bird exhibitors in this country, although only infrequently available, but some of the Asiatic species such as the tiny Black-

2.11 **Mexican Green Jay.** It is difficult to stage large members of the *Corvidae* in perfect plumage. Note fraying to this Jay's tail feathers.

backed Kingfisher (*Ceyx erithacus*) should do equally well in the hands of experienced aviculturists.

Only passing reference has been made in this chapter to the **South American Sugarbirds** (*Dacnidinae*), which, incidentally, are a completely different family to the much more drably-coloured Sugarbirds of Southern Africa (*Promeropidae*). They are, however, generally included in the class for the smaller Tanagers, that is Class L, and are amongst the most striking exhibits with the gorgeous blue plumage of the males in breeding dress. The two most popular species, which are well worthy of a place in any team of Softbills, are the Yellow-winged (*Cyanerpes cyaneus*) and the Purple Sugarbird (*C. caeruleus*).

Class S

All other species of softbills and Nectar Feeders larger in body size than a Pekin Robin

In this final class there is a difficult choice of exhibit because of the range of species involved. Some of the birds which may be entered in this class include, for example, the Jays, Treepies, Touracos, Toucans and Toucanets, Barbets, Drongos, Jay Thrushes, Woodpeckers, Bee-eaters, Hoopoes, Mousebirds or Colies, Rollers, Pittas, Broadbills, Fairy-Bluebird, and a host of others.

It is generally more difficult to stage the larger species in perfect feather condition as their plumage is more liable to damage unless housed in very spacious quarters. Because of this requirement, many exhibitors are unable to provide suitable accommodation for some of these species, with the result that entries of the large species at many open shows is generally very limited in spite of the fact that many of the birds mentioned in the previous paragraph are fairly readily available in this country.

Perhaps one of the most consistently successful groups in this class is the Touraco family (*Musophagidae*) also known as Louries. When staged in perfect condition, the Knysna Touraco (*Tauraco corythaix*) makes a splendid exhibit easily capable of taking top honours in any competition. The rarely imported Cock-of-the-Rock from South America has done well on the show bench, and the equally rare Birds of Paradise, which are as exotic in appearance as any foreign species should look, are also very impressive. These latter species, however, are really only suitable for the connoisseur, and the novice would be well advised to gain experience with the hardier, easy-to-manage species, before attempting to tackle the requirements of the more specialised species.

CHAPTER 3

Obtaining the Birds

DIFFICULTIES INVOLVED IN OBTAINING BIRDS

In order to become an exhibitor of exotic birds, of course, a fancier must own examples of appropriate species. Ownership should be stressed because it is *not* considered fair play to borrow and exhibit birds which belong to another person. Furthermore, the show rules promulgated by many show-promoting societies, stipulate that all exhibits must be the *bona fide* property of the actual exhibitor and, in some cases, must have been in his ownership for a certain period of time prior to the show.

Foreign birds intended for exhibition or breeding (or both) may be obtained in a number of ways. The exhibitor may:

1. **breed suitable specimens from stock already in his possession;**
2. **buy aviary-bred stock from other fanciers;**
3. **buy aviary-bred or wild-caught birds from professional dealers;**
4. **purchase and import wild-caught exotics from their country of origin. This may be difficult and expensive and should only be attempted by the knowledgeable and affluent.**

The fourth method is the one least likely to be employed, as it involves numerous complications, including establishing reliable contacts in the country in question, arranging transport and customs clearance, and, most important of all, providing suitable quarantine facilities for the birds on arrival.

Quarantine Control

There are fairly strict controls governing all quarantine premises, which are subject to inspection by Ministry of Agriculture veterinary inspectors, and it is generally impracticable for most fanciers to provide premises which comply with these requirements. In cases where the fancier is endeavouring to acquire a species which is rarely obtainable in this country he will probably find it easier to arrange for a professional dealer to try and obtain

the birds through his foreign contacts, rather than attempt to carry out the assignment himself.

Aviary-bred specimens of exotic species will normally be available only in the case of those which will breed readily in confinement. This will include many of the Australian Parrakeets and Seedeaters, Diamond Doves, Java Sparrows, Lovebirds, some of the Munias and Waxbills, Quail and a few other assorted species. Many other foreign species, of course, are bred each year but successes are irregular and sporadic, and the availability of such stock, either by purchase or personal endeavour, is largely a matter of chance.

However, as more countries become increasingly conservation conscious and tighter international controls are introduced in an effort to minimise the spread of disease by avian vectors, more and more species are being denied to the aviculturist. It is quite apparent that this situation will escalate in the years ahead and the exhibitor and aviculturist will find fewer and fewer species available at increasing cost.

Solutions

It is therefore, essential that all who are interested in keeping and exhibiting foreign birds, of whatever category, should try and breed regularly from as many of the birds in their possession as accommodation allows. The fancier who breeds even a few foreign finches, for example, is each year contributing far more to the pastime than the exhibitor who spends many pounds on purchasing rare show winners without making any effort to breed from his birds. The breeder/exhibitor will often derive an added bonus from his efforts, because birds bred in confinement from wild-caught stock are often superior in quality to their parents.

METHODS OF ACQUIRING FOREIGN BIRDS

The most common method of acquiring foreign birds is by **purchasing from a professional dealer**. In this country there are scores of dealers who import many thousands of exotic birds each

---

3.1 **Orange-Flanked Parrakeet** (*Brotogeris pyrrhopterus*)
A popular species from South America, this Parrakeet is frequently available and makes a very useful exhibit. It is easy to cater for and has been bred in this country from time to time.

year and, as in all occupations, some are more proficient at their craft than others. There are, however, many reputable dealers who lavish much care and attention on their stock, and it is to these that the prospective purchaser should turn. Buying from a reputable source will ensure that the birds on offer are not only healthy and well cared for, but have also been properly acclimatised or, at least, the proprietor will be willing to advise what stage has been reached in their acclimatisation.

Acclimatisation and Quarantine

The **quarantine requirements** relating to the importation of foreign birds now ensure that freshly imported birds cannot be sold to the public and the importer must, therefore, bear any losses which occur during the crucial first month in this country. It is, however, important that the prospective purchaser should not confuse 'quarantine' with 'acclimatisation'.

In fact, the use of the term 'acclimatised' in relation to imported birds is sometimes misunderstood or, perhaps, incorrectly applied by some retailers. The term literally means 'to become accustomed to a new climate', but, as most readers will be aware, many delicate exotic species are maintained in an artificial climate in this country. It would not, therefore, be realistic to expect that the less hardy species, such as the Humming birds for example, would be acclimatised to withstand the rigours of the British climate in the absence of heating. On the other hand, if those species which are normally kept without the need for heating are described as acclimatised by the vendor, then we would expect them to be accustomed to outdoor or unheated conditions prior to sale.

In practice, however, reputable dealers usually offer acclimatised stock from outdoor or unheated quarters during the summer months, but very few species are obtainable in this state of acclimatisation during the winter. Those who purchase foreign birds during the colder months of the year would, therefore, be well advised not to transfer new stock to unheated quarters unless they are absolutely certain that the birds have been previously accustomed to such conditions.

When the **quarantine regulations** were first promulgated by the authorities, they were regarded with suspicion by some aviculturists as a threat to the pastime of foreign bird keeping. It can be argued however, that these quarantine requirements have benefited both the birds and the birdkeepers.

The Benefits of Quarantine

The fact that importers are obliged to retain their stock for over a month, instead of immediately offering it for sale, means that they will have to bear the cost of any losses which may occur during the quarantine period. It makes economic sense, therefore, that importers should provide the optimum conditions and attention for the newly imported birds in order to reduce such losses to a minimum. Many reputable importers did, of course, provide such conditions for their stock previously, but there were, unfortunately, a few whose main aim appeared to be to push as many birds as possible onto the market as soon as they were unloaded from the aeroplanes. It seems quite certain that the number of deaths among exotic species during the period immediately following importation must have been very high indeed, particularly when these birds were bought by inexperienced fanciers and members of the public.

Although losses still occur, it is probable that foreign birds now receive better treatment from the trade generally than at any time in the past. The imposition of quarantine has, inevitably, resulted in the retail prices for exotic species being considerably increased, although the rises since then are also due in part to general inflation.

It seems certain, however, that most foreign bird enthusiasts are quite happy to pay the increases resulting from the quarantine requirements, in the confident knowledge that the birds being purchased have been screened for any signs of infectious disease, which could otherwise have affected the purchaser's stock.

An additional benefit which has resulted from the introduction of quarantine, and its resultant price rises, is the increase in foreign bird *breeding* as opposed to simply foreign bird *keeping*. It is a sad fact of life that, in the past, when small Waxbills could be purchased for a few shillings, very few fanciers made the effort to try and breed these species. However, now there is some economic potential in breeding foreign birds which has resulted in a much wider range of species receiving the attention of breeders. There has always, of course, been a relatively small number of enthusiasts who have derived satisfaction from breeding even the commonest of foreign birds, such as the Silverbills and Red-Eared Waxbill, which show virtually no financial return. However, at the present time, the prospective purchaser of exotic species will, generally, have to rely on the professional dealer for his stock requirements.

CHOOSING THE BIRD TO BE PURCHASED

Although many dealers will send birds to their customers by rail it is advisable for the inexperienced novice to visit the dealer's establishment so that he may acquire as much information as possible about the birds which he buys. Perhaps the best way for the novice to find the location of his nearest reputable dealer is to attend the meetings of the local cage birds society where experienced fanciers will generally be only too happy to give advice on the subject.

It is perhaps wise to offer a word of warning at this point. Entering the premises of a well-stocked dealer for the first time is, for the budding foreign bird enthusiast, rather like venturing into Aladdin's treasure cave. Some of the avian gems on offer will be very enticing, and the temptation to buy all manner of species will be most compelling. It is essential, however, that the novice should exercise restraint, and purchase only those species for which he can cater adequately.

Suitable accommodation must be available for the birds *before* they are purchased, and the prospective buyer should therefore acquire as much prior knowledge as possible about the requirements of the various species. It is folly, for example, to purchase a pair of Ringneck Parrakeets on the spur of the moment, if the only available accommodation is a Budgerigar-type breeding cage, and yet this has actually been known to occur. The dimensions, and obtainable temperature of the housing facilities available to the fancier must, therefore, govern his choice of species.

Other **limiting factors** will include the 'delicacy' or otherwise of the species, the ability of the fancier to collect, breed and handle live food in the form of insects and larvae, the time available to the fancier for general management, and, of course, the financial resources which he may have at his disposal.

SELECTION OF HEALTHY STOCK

Fortunately, at the present time at least, there is a wide variety of exotic species available to the aviculturist, and some of the hardier and cheaper species are, in any case, also extremely attractive. Whichever species are selected, it is essential that only healthy stock be purchased and that the birds are *potentially* suitable for exhibition.

3.2 **Green-Winged Pigeon** (*Chalcophaps indica*)
Length 10 inches (25.4 cm)
A pleasantly-coloured pigeon from India and the Far East with metallic green wings and mantle and vinaceous-red underparts. It is a quiet species and spends a great deal of time on the ground. Although readily available in this country it is not shown very frequently probably on account of the general difficulty in staging the larger doves and pigeons in immaculate feather.

Healthy birds will be active and bright-eyed with tight plumage. They will be feeding well, and should feel plump and firm when held in the hand. Birds which are huddled together on the perch with eyes shut, plumage fluffed out and *both* feet clutching the perch, should be avoided by the potential purchaser. It will also be noted that sick birds many hop lethargically around the cage floor, picking at odd seeds, or they may be continually at the seed or water pot, and generally looking rather sorry for themselves. This latter behaviour usually indicates that the birds are suffering from gastric disorder, and it will also be frequently observed that the feathers around the birds' vents are soiled by excreta. Birds suffering from **enteritis** will generally have greenish, watery or slimy droppings, with blood occasionally present in the most acute cases.

The inexperienced fancier should never acquire birds showing any of the aforenamed symptoms, as he will almost certainly lose the affected birds, and he may well introduce an infectious disease which could result in the loss of his entire stock. It should be pointed out with regard to the descriptions given above, appertaining to enteric droppings, that these should not be confused with the appearance of the droppings of nectar-feeders and fruit-eating species, which are normally of a very liquid character, or those of many parrot-like birds, which are often green in colour.

ASSESSING EXHIBITION POTENTIAL

As indicated earlier in this chapter when the fancier is buying birds, care should be taken to ensure that they are not only healthy but also potentially suitable for exhibition. What is meant by this, is that the bird must be capable of being brought into perfect show condition by the care and attention of the fancier.

Plumage Damage

It does not give any cause for concern if, at the time of purchase, the tail feathers are broken, or any part of the plumage is broken, missing, frayed or soiled by overcrowded conditions. Provided that the damage to the plumage has not resulted from some physical injury which has also caused permanent damage to the skin below, the missing or defective feathers will be renewed at the next moult.

During importation, when some birds may be subjected to rather crowded conditions, the stress created by such circumstances may

3.3 **An Exhibit of very low Standard.** This **Male Cockatiel**'s tail is frayed and soiled and the condition of his plumage generally is poor. In spite of its appearance this bird is not an example of the Pied Mutation — the extensive pale (yellow) areas of plumage in this instance are possibly due to dietetic deficiency or other physiological aberration. The diameter of the perch is too large for the exhibit's foot size and makes comfortable perching impossible. Although laterally fixed perches, such as this, are popular for parrotlike show cages, they frequently result in the judge finding difficulty in examining the backs and wings of the birds, particularly if the cage front is not angled at the top.

result in a number of species resorting to feather-plucking. Lavender Finches (*Lagonosticta caerulescens*), for example, are particularly prone to this unfortunate trait and, consequently, shipments of this species are generally to be found in a decidedly patchy state of plumage. Provided, however, that no permanent damage has been done to the feather follicles the birds will regain perfect plumage, if suitably housed and managed.

Physical Defects

The prospective purchaser must ensure, of course, that the bird which he proposes to exhibit does not display any physical defect, injury or abnormality. The most important points, which require detailed inspection, are the **feet, beak** and **eyes**.

Feet

Unlike feathers, missing toenails will not grow again, and this fairly common defect can spoil an otherwise excellent exhibit. All species are liable to suffer damage to their feet through various causes but particular attention should be paid to the feet of parrot-like species as they will attack the feet of their own kind when housed in adjoining aviaries. Damage to the tiny claws of the small Waxbills (*Estrilda* spp.), for example, is very difficult to spot when these active little birds are flying around in a dealer's flight or stock cage, and they should be examined in the hand prior to purchase. The dealer will probably prefer to do the holding if his customer is very inexperienced at handling small birds!

Another problem that sometimes occurs is that of overgrown claws, particularly in the case of birds which have been in confinement for a considerable time. Some of the Munias (*Lonchura* spp.) are very liable to this condition: the claws become too long and may catch in wire netting or foliage, resulting in damage to the claws or legs. It is, however, a simple matter to trim off the surplus growth with sharp nail clippers, taking care to avoid cutting into the blood vessel in the claw. If the claw is held up in front of a light, the thin red vein can easily be seen and the claw can then be trimmed carefully to within $^1/_8$th inch (3mm) of the end of the blood vessel. Where necessary, this should be done immediately after purchase, and the claws checked regularly two or three times each year thereafter.

Beaks

Defective beaks are much less common than damaged claws, but occasionally physical injury may leave a permanent defect, or abnormal development of the upper or lower mandible may result in an unnatural elongation which can impair the bird's ability to feed, and will certainly detract from its appearance and show potential. Such birds should not be purchased as exhibition stock, although minor physical damage need not necessarily detract from a bird's potential in the breeding pen.

Eyes

Any permanent physical injury to the eyes will also be readily

3.4 **Pair of White Java Sparrows ruined for exhibition purposes** by the male (bird on the left) having the centre front toe missing from his right foot. Note that the perch has been inserted laterally, in this case to show the bird's foot defect. Normally a pair of birds such as these would be provided with two perches fixed at right angles to the back of the show cage.

apparent to the observer, but blindness may be less easily detected. Fortunately, blindness, other than as a result of external damage to the eye, is fairly rare in the case of foreign species, but the eyes should, nevertheless, be examined for any signs of abnormality. Grey Singing Finches (*Serinus leucopygia*), for example, are very liable to inflammation of the eyes, although the condition can be remedied by treatment.

The intending exhibitor must, of course, also consider other factors when assessing the show potential of the birds which he is selecting.

Size

As stated in Chapter 9, many judges appear to consider that quality is synonymous with size. In other words, they adopt the adage that a 'good, big 'un' will beat a 'good, little 'un'. Whatever the

3.5 **A nicely matched pair of White Java Sparrows** (*Padda oryzivora*). These birds are fairly easy to keep in good condition but often have to compete in rarer species of their class.

fanciers' views may be on the subject, it is a fact that not many red cards will be won at shows by birds smaller than the other exhibits.

SELECTING A BIRD OF MORE COMMON SPECIES

When visiting the establishment of one of the larger dealers, the prospective buyer will generally discover that there are scores, or even hundreds, of examples of each of the commoner species from which to choose. It is usually found that if the fancier takes along a suitable show cage when buying birds, the dealer will catch several examples which can be more closely examined in the show cage. With the co-operation of a helpful dealer, good, representative examples of the species of suitable substance and quality can be selected in this way.

When dealing with small foreign seedeaters and some parrot-like species, it is normal practice to exhibit the birds in *true pairs*. It is essential that these pairs should be well matched with regard to size, colour and plumage pattern, and the use of a show cage at the dealer's establishment is useful for comparing various specimens in order to select the most suitable partners.

CHAPTER 4

Housing

SIZE AND DESIGN

A wide variety of accommodation is used to house exotic birds in this country, ranging from the huge walk–through aviaries to be seen at commercial zoological and bird gardens to the simple box cage in a back garden shed or spare room.

Obviously the size and design of the accommodation (and, therefore, the type of birds which can be kept) will be governed by the amount of land available to the fancier and, of course, the condition of his bank account. Fairly specialised conditions may be required for some species; one of the most unusual and effective designs to be seen in this country, is the Seashore Aviary at Bird World, near Farnham in Surrey. This high, spacious aviary, landscaped with rocks and sandy beach, even has a wave-making machine, which creates an uncannily–realistic, constant succession of waves breaking on the shoreline. The Cormorants, Terns, Waders and other seabirds which share this elaborate accommodation look completely at ease with their surroundings.

This is not to suggest, of course, that the average aviculturist should try to emulate such perfect conditions, relatively few could afford to do so, but it is advantageous to provide conditions for the various species as similar as possible to whose, which they would encounter in the wild.

STOCK CAGES

Many of the smaller species can be kept in good health and condition in box–type cages in the birdroom for several years, but there is little chance of achieving successful *breeding* results under such conditions, except in the case of those species which are partially–domesticated, such as some of the Australian grassfinches.

4.1 **A block of roomy stock cages** housing a selection of British-bred Australian Grassfinches. The vertical slots allow the insertion of partition slides to convert the cages to individual breeding compartments for appropriate species. Water supply in plastic drinking fountains at perch level prevents its contamination by droppings. Note also the removable sand trays in the bottom of the cages to facilitate cleaning.

It is fairly obvious that accommodation of limited size will become fouled more quickly and will therefore require more frequent cleaning. This is particularly true in the case of softbills, where the generally soft and sticky characteristics of their foodstuffs, and the liquid and often copious nature of their droppings can result in floors, perches and cage fronts becoming quickly fouled. If such conditions are allowed to occur, the plumage of the birds will soon become soiled and damaged and they will be utterly useless from an exhibition viewpoint.

Some fanciers may, however be obliged by circumstances to house their stock in cages, and this need not deter them from enjoying the hobby of exhibiting. In fact, I myself, use outside breeding flights without shelters for some of my birds during the summer months, and then bring the less hardy species into the birdroom for the winter, housing them in cages and indoor flights.

It is essential that stock cages should be as roomy as possible to allow the inmates ample exercise. It is impossible to stipulate an optimum size for every foreign species and, of course, there are some species that are totally unsuited to cage life, requiring properly designed aviary accommodation. I would strongly suggest, however, that the minimum cage dimensions acceptable for housing non–domesticated foreign species would be 30 inches (76·2 cm) long × 15 inches (38·1 cm) × 15 inches. A cage of this size would provide adequate non–breeding accommodation for a pair of Waxbills, Singing Finches, Zosterops or other seedeaters or softbills of similar size.

For larger species the size of the cage should be increased accordingly and dimensions of 48 inches (1·22 m) long × 24 inches (61 cm) high × 15 inches (38·1 cm) wide would, for example, be an adequate minimum for species such as Bulbuls and Fruitsuckers.

It is a useful idea to construct stock cages in blocks of, say, twelve, with removable sliding partitions between each cage. This provides an element of flexibility, so that a row of three 30 inch (76·2 cm) cages can be instantly converted to a flight cage 7 feet 6 inches (2·29 m) in length.

Perches and Food Receptacles

Some thought must also be given to the design and positioning of perches and food receptacles. It is preferable to use natural twigs, rather than rigid dowel for perching, as this will present a variety of diameters and angles, which provide beneficial exercise for the birds' feet. The perches should be positioned in such a way that the birds can perch comfortably with their heads quite clear of the cage roof, and their tails in no danger of becoming frayed through contact with the end of the cage or any other obstruction.

Food and water vessels should be positioned in such a way that they do not become fouled by droppings from birds on the perches. In the case of most Softbills and some of the long-tailed Seedeaters, such as the Viduine Whydahs, it is advisable to secure the food vessels at perch height to minimise unnecessary soiling of the birds' plumage by floor debris, while they are feeding.

AVIARIES

Although cages provide a fairly satisfactory method of housing many foreign species, there is little doubt that aviaries of various designs are to be preferred in most instances. Bascially, of course, an aviary is simply a large cage, but the increased space available offers a number of benefits to both the birds and the fancier.

The larger aviaries can be landscaped, and even quite small flights can be planted with suitable vegetation, provided that the species to be housed are not too destructive to plant life. The provision of shrubs and flowering plants in an aviary serves a threefold purpose. A tastefully planted aviary can be an attractive feature of the garden with, for example, climbing plants, such as clematis or honeysuckle, used to soften the angular outline which such a structure generally presents. The ornamental garden aviary does, apart from any other consideration, afford its owner the opportunity to spend many fascinating hours observing his birds behaving almost completely naturally in pleasant surroundings.

The use of natural features has two additional advantages, which are even more important than the aesthetic effects from the point of view of the serious aviculturist. Quite a number of foreign species can be bred in "unfurnished" functional flights or aviaries, but many others must be provided with realistically natural conditions if success is to be achieved. A well planted aviary not only offers privacy and protection from the elements for the inmates, but also provides the actual sites for nest construction.

Planting an aviary

When planting an aviary with breeding in mind, some thought must be given as to which species are to be kept. The aviculturist must endeavour to obtain information about his birds' requirements with regard to their natural selection of nesting materials and locations. It is important to know whether a particular species nests at ground level, in cavities, or constructs its nest in shrubs or other vegetation; or, indeed, whether it is a brood parasitic like the Viduine Whydahs.

Some species, in fact, have very specialised requirements in the way of nesting locations, which must be simulated, if not reproduced exactly, if the birds are to be encouraged to nest. The Red-faced Lovebird (*Agapornis pullaria*) for example, constructs its nesting chamber in the wild by tunnelling into the huge nests of termites which occur in the West African savanna.

Although the Red-faced Lovebird has been bred on a few occasions in captivity, using bales of peat in lieu of termite's nests, it is

4.2 **A Garden Aviary**

scarcely surprising that it remains one of the least commonly available Lovebirds in this country. Some of the *Ploceus* and *Euplectes* Weavers from Southern Africa, build their pendulous nests suspended over water, while others, like the Red Bishop (*Euplectes orix*), nest in reed beds at the water margin. Obviously, if an attempt is to be made to breed these species, or others with similar requirements, some form of pool or water feature should be incorporated in the aviary layout.

The examples I have quoted are some of the more specialised cases, but they serve to illustrate the need to study the particular requirements of one's birds when considering the provision of suitable housing. Some exotic species are very destructive to growing plants and shrubs, and in such instances, of course, it is generally a waste of effort and expense trying to provide vegetation in the aviary. Most of the Parrot family fall within this category and with such birds it is advisable to provide only adequate branches for climbing and perching. These will have to be renewed frequently as they will be destroyed by the birds' powerful beaks, most Parrots being enthusiastic chewers of woodwork. The floors of Parrot aviaries may be grass, gravel or concrete. Grass floors can, of course, become overgrown and tangled if not regularly tended, and grass–cutting can cause disruption in the aviary while the birds are breeding.

A third advantage, which may be derived from planting the aviary, relates principally to those species whose diet includes insects. Although exotic species are generally divided by aviculturists into the two loosely–defined categories of Softbills and Seedeaters, many birds from both groups will in fact require a partially–insectivorous diet. This is particularly true of many Seedeaters when they are rearing nestlings, and most of the Waxbills, for example, can only be successfully bred when suitable livefood is available.

The larger, insect–eating species, such as Starlings, Thrushes, and so on can be catered for to a considerable extent by supplying mealworms, gentles, locusts and other cultivated livefoods. These may be bred by the aviculturist or are readily purchased from dealers. This type of livefood, however, is too large and tough for Waxbills and other small species which require an insect element in their diet.

In an outdoor aviary, therefore, it is a considerable advantage to

4.3 **Great White Cockatoo** (*Cacatua cristata*)
The largest of the cockatoos; only rarely available to aviculturists. A native of the Mollucan Islands, it requires very strongly–constructed accommodation, as a conventional aviary will rapidly be demolished by its powerful beak. Also known as the Umbrella Cockatoo.

attract naturally–occurring insect life into the flight. Few insects will be drawn to a bare, featureless aviary with concrete floor, but the inclusion of shrubs and flowering plants will certainly encourage their presence. In other parts of the garden, aphids may be undesirable pests, but in the aviary they constitute a valuable supplement to the diet of the inmates. The type of vegetation to be planted will obviously be governed by the size of the enclosure, the nature of the soil and the location of the aviary, but only those plants should be selected which will flourish without frequent attention by the fancier during the summer months, otherwise disturbance to nesting birds may occur.

Aviary Size and Design

The actual size and design of the aviary will, of course, be governed by the choice of species which one intends housing in it. It is preferable, indeed it is virtually essential, to err on the side of generosity when allocating aviary space to one's birds, if perfect condition is to be maintained. For this reason one should never obtain additions to one's stock unless suitable accommodation exists, or can be provided within a short time.

Individual or communal design
The first question which the fancier must decide is whether he prefers to house his birds in a communal aviary or in individual compartments each containing one pair or a small colony of the same species. In the former type of establishment, only compatible species should be housed together. This is particularly important when it is intended to exhibit the birds during the show season, as even minor squabbling can result in damage to plumage or claws which will ruin the bird's potential as an exhibit for the season at least. In addition, of course, constant aggression between the different species will seriously jeopardise breeding results.

Fortunately there is a fairly wide choice of species which are compatible given adequate space and facilities. Size can be used as a rough, but not infallible, guide when selecting aviary companions. Most of the Waxbills, for example, will live quite amicably together, along with the smaller Munias. Larger species, such as Java Sparrows, and the various Australian Grassfinches should not, as a rule, be included with the smaller Seedeaters as they can be rather aggressive on occasion.

Housing the species
Occasionally one may see advice given to the question as to which exotic species may be safely housed with **Budgerigars** in a communal aviary. The advice generally includes such species as Java Sparrows, Weavers, Whydahs and Cut-throat Finches. Why this last–named species should ever have been suggested as a suitable companion for Budgerigars baffles me! I can only assume that some well–meaning author, misled by the bird's somewhat villainous name, presumed it to be a particularly aggressive species, and other advisers have continued to profer the same advice unquestioningly. The Cutthroat Finch, frequently ignored because of its ready availability and low cost, is in fact a delightful exhibit for the Common Seedeater section and can safely be housed with Mannikins, Singing Finches and similar species. It should be emphasised, of course, when considering aggression, that, as in most animal species, temperament varies with the individual. Conse-

4.4 **Male Chinese Necklace Dove** (*Streptopelia chinesis*) — a widespread Asiatic species which may safely be housed with other species. The larger Doves are difficult to stage in perfect feather.

quently, although one may regard a particular species as being quite docile, it is always possible for certain individuals of that species to display aggressive tendencies which would render them unsuitable for inclusion in a communal aviary.

To revert to the question of housing Budgerigars with exotic species, I would suggest that the only really suitable companions for Budgerigars are more Budgerigars. Certainly, the larger species of Weavers, Cardinals, and so on, will be able to fend for themselves in a Budgerigar aviary, but in these circumstances one is creating a situation of armed neutrality rather than compatibility. The constant sparring and bickering will generally make it difficult to maintain the birds in perfect show condition. Having kept Budgerigars with various foreign species in the past, I have witnessed some very nasty and unwarranted assaults by bad–tempered hen Budgerigars, in particular, on their aviary companions, and would strongly recommend that Budgerigars be housed in separate quarters.

Parrot–like birds generally are best housed on the basis of one pair to each flight. This is essential when breeding and is also advisable when housing exhibition stock. There are a few exceptions to the general rule, of course, and some of the Lovebirds have been bred fairly successfully on the colony system, although even with these it is preferable to house them, one pair per enclosure. A further point, which should be borne in mind where Parrot–like species are housed in adjoining flights, is that some of these birds have a tendency to bite the feet of their neighbours when they alight on the intervening wire partition. This can result in injury which can ruin a bird's exhibition potential, and in such situations it is advisable to ensure that partitions between the flights are double–wired, that is, two layers of wire mesh with a gap of at least 1 inch (25·4 mm) between.

The housing of **Softbills** is, perhaps, a more complex subject because of the wider divergence of behaviour patterns. Insectivorous and fruit–eating species tend to display a greater degree of territorial aggression than most seed–eating birds. Their territories, both in the wild and in confinement, are more clearly defined and are relatively extensive in area. Furthermore, the territories of many such species are not only defined for breeding purposes but also serve to encompass suitable sources of food supply. Consequently the territory will be defended for the whole of the year and not only during the breeding season. In fact, it will be found with some insectivorous species that, while a pair share the same territory amicably during the summer months and breed successfully, one or other of the birds will not tolerate its mate's presence outside the breeding season and will harass it unmercifully.

In the case of the vast majority of fanciers it will generally be true to say that the average aviary will only be of sufficient size to provide feeding territory for a single bird or breeding territory for one pair, when territorially aggressive species are to be housed. It is, of course, frequently possible to house several different non–competing species in the same aviary, provided it is of suitable size, and a pair of Tanagers, for example, could share their accommodation with the ground–frequenting Pittas. In addition, economical utilisation of aviary space can also be achieved by housing some of the seed–eating species in the Softbill aviaries. The Seedeaters generally benefit from such an arrangement because of the wider range of foodstuffs usually available, often of a high protein nature. Small birds of any species should never, of course, be housed with any of the larger predatory softbills such as Magpies, Cissas and similar species.

It will be apparent, therefore, that the provision of suitable accommodation for Softbills should always be given careful consideration and forethought. While the size of the birds may have some limited value in deciding on suitable companions in the case of unrelated species, it is quite irrelevant in instances of intraspecific aggression or territorial defence against closely–related species. The family which provides the world's smallest bird, also contains some of the most aggressive: the Humming birds (*Trochilidae*). These tiny, feathered gems are so aggressive towards their own kind that they can rarely be accommodated together except in the huge, lush tropical houses of commercial bird gardens and, even when being exhibited for a couple of days, the Humming birds can normally only be shown as a pair if the show cage is effectively divided into two separate compartments by a vertical partition.

When designing flights for territorially–aggressive species, therefore, it is preferable to have, for example, two flights each 12 feet (3·66 m) × 4 feet (1·22 m) rather than a single flight 12 feet (3·66 m) × 8 feet (2·44 m). If breeding is to be contemplated two adjoining flights can be made in such a way that they can be rapidly converted to a single, larger enclosure by removing or folding one of the partition panels. This allows male and female of aggressive species to be housed separately outside the breeding season, but within sight and sound of each other.

Construction

Aviary construction can be as simple or as elaborate as the fancier's desires and cheque book dictate. The majority of aviculturists, however, purchase or build a structure comprising of a timber framework covered in galvanised wire mesh as the open flight area, with an attached shelter of close–boarded wooden construction. Alternatively, the flights may be attached to a larger birdroom with interconnecting indoor compartments, which has the added advantage that any particularly delicate species may be readily confined within the birdroom during prolonged periods of inclement weather. It is surprising, in fact, how many species of tropical birds will not only tolerate, but actually appear to enjoy outdoor life during our winter months. No imported bird should be subjected to spartan conditions of weather, of course, until it has been properly acclimatised.

It may sometimes be impossible to construct outdoor flights adjacent to the birdroom because of garden layout or other limiting topographical features, and in such instances a compromise can be achieved by constructing a range of individual breeding flights (without shelters) which can be used during the Spring to Autumn season only, with the birds being transferred into indoor accommodation in the birdroom for the Winter. I have used this system myself and find it perfectly satisfactory; and it has the advantage that the breeding flights can be thoroughly cleaned out and rested during the winter.

Although this volume has been specifically written to provide information for the foreign bird exhibitor (or potential exhibitor), I am firmly of the belief that it is reprehensible to keep exotic species and not attempt to breed from them. Consequently, when discussing housing or any other aspect of foreign bird culture it is assumed in this book, that the exhibitor will also wish to try and breed from his birds during the spring and summer months, and any advice offered, therefore, will, where practicable, be of a dual purpose nature.

A number of basic factors must be taken into account when designing aviary accommodation and, first of all, the traditional timber/wire mesh structure will be dealt with.

Vermin

The aviary must, as far as possible, be vermin–proof. It is quite difficult, and expensive, to make any form of building completely proof against entry by rodents, and the bird seed and other foods in an aviary can, of course, be a source of attraction to rats and mice. Young mice can quite easily make their way through the ½-inch (13 mm) mesh wire netting which is normally used in aviary construction; and even if ³/₈ inch (9.5 mm) mesh is used, the smallest gap in the woodwork will provide access for a mouse.

Apart from the fact that mice can contaminate the birds' foodsstuffs with their droppings and urine, they can also upset breeding birds and are quite capable of killing nestlings. They must, there-

fore, be strictly controlled if they should become established in an aviary, and traps and anti–coagulant poisons must be used in an effort to eradicate them. "Break–back", or any other form of mechanical traps and poisons must, of course, never be situated in the aviary itself, or in any position where the birds can obtain access to them. If traps or poisons are placed inside lengths of drainpipe and located outside the wall of the aviary they should be quite effective and inaccessible to pets and wild birds.

Rats are a somewhat difficult and more serious threat. In addition to possessing all the most undesirable qualities of mice, they are also perfectly capable of attacking, killing and eating adult birds. They cannot penetrate sound ½-inch mesh (13 mm) wire–netting, however, but they can and will tunnel underneath the walls of the aviary unless precautions are taken to prevent them. This can usually be achieved by extending the wire netting of the flight walls below the level of the adjoining ground for a depth of approximately 6–9 inches (15–23 cm) and then turning it outwards so that it extends out from the base of the flight for some 12 inches (30·5 cm) or so. It is, of course, necessary to dig a shallow trench around the base of the aviary during the construction to enable this to be done. The same effect can be achieved using bricks and/or concrete although this will probably be more expensive.

Although ½-inch mesh wire is generally used to cover flights, which are to house the smaller species, there is a temptation to use 1-inch (25 mm) mesh or even larger when accommodating larger birds, due to the lower cost. The larger mesh will, of course, keep the birds in but it will not keep out rats, mice, weasels, sparrows and other creatures which might have evil designs on the inmates, their nestlings, or their food supply.

Design for larger birds

The larger Parrots, Cockatoos and Macaws are quite capable of biting through standard gauge wire mesh with their powerful beaks, as well as demolishing the woodwork of their aviaries, and, in their case, flights of more robust construction are necessary. Aviaries for these birds are, therefore, often constructed of angle–iron covered with chain-link wire netting.

4.5 **A useful range of breeding flights** for spring to autumn use, when one pair of birds is housed in each compartment. Note the low entrance doors to minimise risk of escapees.

Safety porch

One of the problems which frequently arises is the possibility of birds escaping as one enters the aviary, and this is probably more of a risk in the case of smaller enclosures where the birds cannot get too far away from the entrance as their keeper approaches. Also, of course, where tame and fearless individuals are concerned they will often move towards the fancier as he enters their compartment. The ideal solution to the problem is to provide a safety porch over the entrance to the flight. This would normally comprise of a small wire-mesh covered cubicle, approximately 3 feet (91 cm) square, constructed adjacent to the aviary entrance door, designed so that the fancier can enter the safety porch and close the door behind him before opening the aviary door.

The construction of a safety porch does, of course, add to the cost of the aviary, and if a range of flights is involved this may be quite daunting. If a single valuable bird is lost, however, because of the absence of a safety porch, it assumes a different aspect, unfortunately, with hindsight. A compromise can be achieved, without incurring the expense of safety porches, by ensuring that the entrance doors to the flights are restricted in height to not more than about 3 feet (91 cm), with a width of around 2 feet (61 cm). Doors of these dimensions may pose some problem for the less agile fancier, but there is very little risk of birds flying out over your head on entering the flight.

Shelter compartment

Where a shelter compartment is to be attached to the flight, it must be soundly constructed to exclude draughts and rainwater. Many acclimatised exotic species can withstand quite low temperatures, certainly well below freezing point, provided that they can occupy dry, draught–free quarters at night, and such hardy species will not require artificial heating provided that their shelters are well–insulated. It is also important to ensure that the shelter is well–lit as birds are generally reluctant to enter dark surroundings (except next–boxes and similar cavities, of course), and they may have to spend considerable periods in the shelter during inclement weather. Glass windows in the shelter should always be covered with wire mesh to prevent escapes in the event of accidental breakage of the glass. Although adequate natural lighting is essential, it is also advisable to take precautions against the birds being over–exposed to too much direct sunlight through the glass, perhaps by

4.6 **Parrakeet Aviaries in a pleasant Garden Setting.** Individual shelters are provided at the rear of each flight for feeding and roosting during inclement weather. Heating is generally unnecessary as most parrakeets are extremely hardly once acclimatised. Fairly long flights are required for these active, swift flying species.

positioning the shelter window on a north–facing wall.

The entrance aperture, or bobhole, to the shelter should be large enough to allow the birds easy, unhindered access, but not so extensive that it nullifies the purpose of the shelter by allowing the ingress of the elements. The actual dimensions will, like the size of the enclosure, be governed by the species accommodated. A sliding, or hinged flap should be provided to the bobhole so that the birds can be confined in the shelter when necessary.

Conservatory/greenhouse aviary

A question that is frequently asked, particularly by beginners, is whether a garden greenhouse or conservatory can be used to house exotic birds. These structures can certainly be used for this purpose, but they are not wholly satisfactory and have certain disadvantages.

Because of the large area of glass involved, the interior of the conservatory–type aviary is subject to extremes of temperature induced by prevailing weather conditions. It is, therefore, necessary to achieve a reasonable degree of temperature control, which can result in rather expensive heating bills during the colder months. Fanciers will no doubt be aware that the natural variation between midday temperatures and those after nightfall in many tropical countries is quite considerable, and birds from these regions will, of course, be accustomed to fairly sudden and dramatic drops in after–dark temperatures.

The conservatory/greenhouse aviary lends itself admirably to planting in a manner which is impossible with a wire–mesh covered outdoor flight. Exotic tropical vegetation can be used to create conditions which perfectly complement the birds and which also results in a more humid atmosphere than can otherwise be obtained. If birds and plants are to thrive during the bleak winter months it is essential that artificial heating and lighting be provided. Electric tubular heaters which can be thermostatically controlled are probably the most convenient method of heating the smaller conservatory aviary although electricity costs are rather high in relation to some other methods. Oil heaters require more attention and great care is necessary to ensure that smoke and fumes are not allowed to develop which would rapidly kill birds and vegetation.

Because of the extremely high temperatures which can occur on very hot summer days, the conservatory aviary must be provided with adequate means of ventilation and, of course, all openings must be covered in small diameter wire–mesh. If fine wire gauze is used instead of normal wire–mesh, this will also serve to contain any live insects which may be released into the aviary as food for the inhabitants.

When birds are first released into this type of aviary, care should be taken, for a few days, that they are not alarmed or suddenly disturbed in any way as they are liable to dash against the glass and injuries may occur. A removable colourwash type of paint can be used to indicate the existence of glass to the birds, and it may be necessary to continue partial use of this to provide some shade later.

The "tropical jungle" conditions, which the conservatory aviary can provide may be very pleasing to the human eye, but they are not appreciated by all exotic species. Certainly species which originate from low–lying humid regions will thrive under these conditions, but those from semi–arid or high altitude habitats will, in most cases, do better in the outdoor wire–mesh type of flight. It is, therefore, advisable that the conservatory aviary and the Softbill species, which it probably suits best, be left to the more experienced fancier.

CHAPTER 5

Show Condition

FITNESS

As suggested in Chapter 8, **condition** is the most important factor to be considered when judging exotic birds, or indeed any other form of livestock. Unlike breeding condition, in which the superficial appearance of the bird is unimportant, show condition necessitates that every aspect of the exhibit's physical condition must, ideally, be flawless.

Obviously, all birds intended for exhibition must be free of disease and, of course, any birds which have been in contact with a sick bird should not be shown until they are known to be free of the disease, particularly if it is of the contagious variety. Birds, which are suffering from acute illnesses, can generally be readily identified as such by the various symptoms which may be apparent. The sick bird will usually be huddled on the perch, or in the seed dish, with fluffed out plumage and eyes closed, and may also show such symptoms as loose, slimy, green or blood-stained droppings and laboured, noisy breathing. However, the causal organism can also be present in apparently healthy birds during the incubation period of the disease, and may persist in previously sick birds which have recovered and no longer show any external symptoms. For this reason it would be irresponsible to allow any bird, which was likely to be in an infectious condition, to appear at a show, thereby putting at risk hundreds, or even thousands, of valuable birds.

Fitness, of course, does not simply mean being free of disease, and the exhibition bird should be well nurtured but clean-cut and devoid of obesity. Birds which are too fat tend to be lethargic, and seldom show to advantage. The major cause of obesity in exotic species is usually a combination of unsuitable diet and restricted accommodation.

5.1 **Typical all-metal Hospital Cage** — a removable glass front in front of the metal bars retains the heat and eliminates draughts. Heat is provided by the thermostatically-controlled electrical element beneath the cage floor. Heat is an essential factor in the treatment of sick birds; note the thermometer to ensure that sufficiently high temperature is being maintained. Hospital cages are sometimes used to dry off birds which have been hand-washed for exhibition purposes but great care is necessary to prevent the risk of cross-infection from previous occupants.

NUTRITIONAL REQUIREMENTS

The majority of open shows are held during the months of September to December, so that the show season is getting under way just as the breeding season, for most foreign species, is drawing to a close. Most fanciers are aware that the process of rearing youngsters imposes a considerable strain on the resources of the parent birds, and it is, therefore, evident that birds, which have been subjected to the rigours of breeding, should be allowed to recuperate and regain full fitness before being exposed to the further stresses of exhibiting. During this period of recuperation following breeding it is essential that the birds' nutritional requirements are met to the full, particularly as this time usually coincides with the annual moult, when the frayed, work-worn feathers are replaced with a completely new set of plumage. After breeding, the bird's bodily reserves of essential vitamins, minerals and other dietary constituents will be low, so that any shortfall in the diet may well affect the quality of the new plumage.

During the moult, the birds should not be exhibited and must be allowed complete rest, while, at the same time a protein-rich diet should be supplied, For example, in the case of the **Seedeaters**, the oil seeds are an invaluable addition to the diet, and such seeds as niger, linseed, hemp and sunflower can be offered, depending on the size of the species in question. In addition to their higher protein composition, these seeds also have a high oil content and are therefore a good supplement for all Seedeaters throughout the winter months. Although it is advisable to be generous with the oil seeds during the moult, it is better to cut back on the quantities offered when the moult has been completed as the birds may put on too much fat, particularly if housed in stock cages rather than aviaries.

The **Softbills** (a fanciers' term for all those species other than Seedeaters), as a general rule require a much higher protein content in their basic diet than those species which subsist mainly on seeds and vegetable matter. Protein is composed of amino-acids in varying combinations and, consequently, varies in character and properties. In other words, if one type of protein was lacking a particular, essential amino-acid, then a diet comprised of that type of protein in whatever quantity would still be deficient. Variety, therefore, is a useful safety factor in any diet as it spreads the probability of supplying all the essential ingredients. Care should also be taken, in the case of insectivorous and omnivorous species, to include an element of animal protein in the diet rather than just vegetable protein.

In addition to ensuring that a protein-rich diet is offered during the moult and prior to the show season, it is essential that the **vitamin** content of the diet is not overlooked. Although many foodstuffs, which can be supplied to various species, are a valuable source of some of the vitamins it is difficult to ensure that any bird's vitamin requirements are being wholly met in this way. I believe

Plate 1 Foreign Birds

Plate 2 Foreign Birds

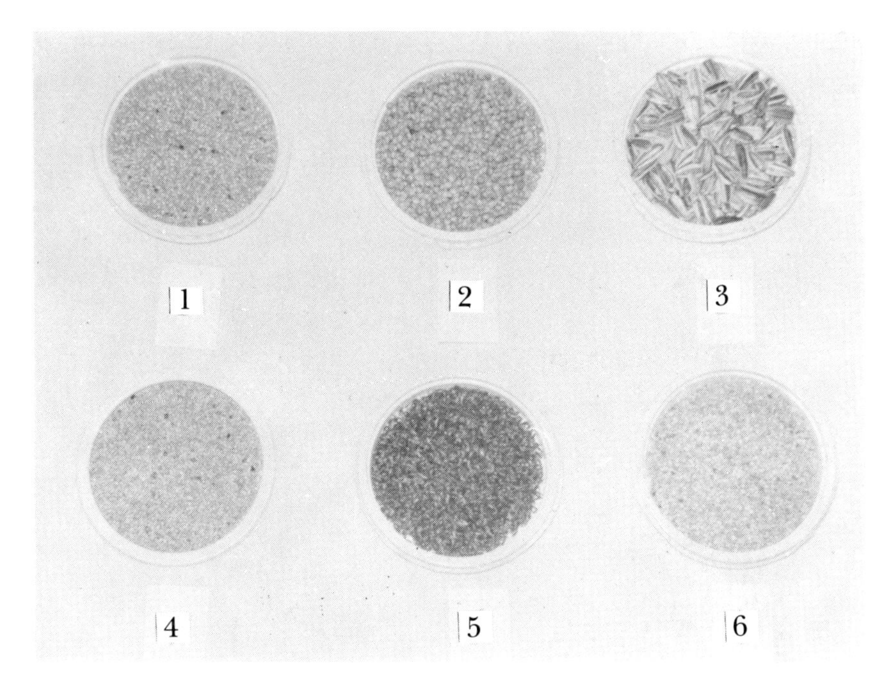

5.2 **Selection of seeds suitable for various foreign species:**
1. Plain canary
2. Hemp
3. Striped sunflower
4. Pannicum millet
5. Niger
6. Mixed millets (including Plate, White and Pannicum)

Hemp, Sunflower and Niger all have a relatively high oil content and should be offered with discretion particularly in the case of the smaller species.

that it is advantageous to supply all the necessary vitamins 'from the bottle', particularly during periods of critical metabolic activity such as growth, moult and breeding. Vitamin supplements are available in powder, tablet and liquid form, but, my personal opinion is that the most satisfactory method is to supply a multi-vitamin solution by drops added to the birds' drinking water or nectar mixture, if the latter is being offered. Incidentally, a nectar solution is itself a beneficial supplement for seedeaters and other species, as well as nectar-feeders, but in the case of the former, it should be strictly rationed as it can result in digestive problems if the birds partake too liberally. Although the use of a powdered vitamin supplement on seed is not recommended, such additives can readily be mixed with soft food and insectivorous mixtures and can be fed satisfactorily in this way. Vitamins in tablet form are not really suitable for feeding to birds, for obvious reasons.

Diet will not be discussed in greater depth in these notes as it is a wide-ranging and complex subject, but those who are interested, will find a chapter devoted to nutrition (mainly relative to seedeaters) in *The Bengalese Finch**. The subject has been touched on lightly here, to emphasise to the fancier that conditioning for exhibition does not merely commence a few weeks before a show, but is a long-term process which is in some respects dependent on the dietary treatment of stock before, during and after the breeding season.

MAINTAINING FITNESS

One of the factors which frequently results in an exhibit being left out of the cards is a condition known as 'softness'. This somewhat vague term is probably best defined as being the antithesis of fitness. In other words, a bird which is 'soft' is out of condition and has lost the tight-feathered, keen edge of physical well-being. Softness may result from:

1. **obesity**
2. **ailments**
3. **debility after breeding**
4. **irregular application of artificial lighting and heating.**

It is the last-mentioned factor which will be dealt with here.

Heating and Lighting

Newcomers to birdkeeping are frequently surprised to find that some exotic species can be successfully maintained in temperate climes without the provision of heating in winter. These conditions, of course, may only be applied to the hardier species, and then only when they have been properly acclimatised or are aviary-bred.

It is, however, essential that our few hours of winter daylight are extended by artificial means where small exotic species are being housed. Although such tiny creatures as Red-eared Waxbills will withstand sub-zero temperatures with no ill effects, they cannot be expected to endure almost sixteen hours of darkness when they are unable to feed, as may occur in December to January. The provi-

*J. Buchan: published by Isles d'Avon (1976)

5.3 **Electrically controlled time switch**: useful in operating the artificial lighting automatically. Where electric lighting is used to extend the natural hours of daylight for exotic species, it is essential that it be carefully and consistently regulated.

sion of **electric lighting** is, therefore, an essential element in the successful management of foreign birds, but it is one which requires careful consideration.

Most fanciers are aware that it is the lengthening hours of daylight in Spring which trigger a bird's instinct to commence its breeding cycle. This light-controlled mechanism thus ensures that breeding takes place at the most favourable time, when the length of the days and the supplies of chick-rearing foodstuffs are at their peak. Birds which are housed indoors can be induced to come into breeding condition earlier than Nature intended by careful manipulation of artificial lighting, gradually extending the hours of light in a controlled facsimile of approaching Spring, but much earlier. This practice is commonly adopted by Budgerigar breeders who have, nowadays, brought forward early breeding to the stage where their first-hatched chicks are ready to be close-rung when the rings are issued by the specialist societies at the beginning of January.

Although, therefore, artificial lighting can be of great benefit to bird and fancier alike if properly utilised, it can create undesirable side effects when used haphazardly. If, for example, the hour of darkness is varied indiscriminately — say six o'clock one evening, nine o'clock for a couple of nights and then back to seven o'clock — birds may develop signs of softness or begin shedding odd feathers in a 'soft moult'.

Heating can also create problems for the exhibitor. Many aviculturists maintain their foreign birds during the winter in quarters where the minimum temperature is kept at a few degrees above freezing point. However, at many show venues the temperature during the afternoon will frequently rise to 22°C (68°F) or more as the hall becomes crowded, and it may be found that exhibits returning from such conditions will commence a 'soft moult' which can prevent their being shown for a number of weeks. There is little the exhibitor can do to counteract this problem except to exhort the show organisers to try and maintain temperatures at a reasonable level in the show venue, although, obviously, this is virtually impossible in many show halls.

PLUMAGE

One further aspect of show condition which sometimes causes confusion to exhibitors is the matter of **eclipse plumage**. Most fanciers are aware that, in the case of a considerable number of species, the males develop **breeding plumage** at the commencement of the nesting season. This nuptial finery is completely different from the generally dowdy feathering which is worn outside the breeding season (the eclipse plumage), and in addition usually comprises bright, striking pigmentation with, in some cases, new forms of feather structure. The females do not acquire this conspicuous garb because of the need for obscurity during the vulnerable incubation period.

In avicultural terms, the exotic species of interest to the exhibitor which assume breeding plumage are the Whydahs, many of the Weavers, Sugarbirds and Sunbirds, and the Red Avadavat or Tiger

Finch (*Amandava amandava*). This last-named species, is, in fact, the only Waxbill which adopts breeding plumage.

It is normal practice for most dealers, when offering Weavers and Whydahs for sale in advertisements, to describe the state of their plumage by the following abbreviations:

1. **O.O.C.** — Out of colour; i.e., in eclipse plumage.
2. **C.I.C.** — Coming into colour; i.e., with partially-developed breeding plumage.
3. **I.F.C.** — In full colour; i.e., with fully-developed breeding plumage.

The prices asked for birds described as O.O.C. are usually less than those in the other two categories, but there is, of course, the risk in such circumstances that the purchaser may obtain two females instead of a true pair, as the eclipse plumage of both sexes is very similar in many instances.

SHOWING AND THE STATE OF PLUMAGE

As the majority of open bird shows are held, in this country, during the period from the beginning of September to the end of December, it will, of course, be apparent that the wearing of full breeding plumage will not coincide with our show season in the case of all the aforementioned species. The question then arises as to whether it is permissible to exhibit these species when the males are out of colour or coming into colour.

There are no rules or regulations which require that only birds in *full colour* may be exhibited, although it is common practice that this should be the case. There is no practical reason why one should not exhibit a pair of Weavers, for example, of which the male is in eclipse plumage. It is, of course, a perfectly natural condition for the bird to be in and in any event, the aim is not to select the bird with the prettiest colours!

It could be argued with some justification in the case of the Whydahs that males in full breeding dress should be given preference, as maintaining the exceptionally long tail feathers, which most of them develop, in perfect condition requires greater skill on the part of the exhibitor, than would be the case if the birds were in eclipse plumage. This argument cannot, however, be applied to some of the other species concerned and there is, therefore no valid reason why males in eclipse dress should not be entered in show.

With birds which are just coming into colour, i.e., in the process of developing their breeding plumage, the situation is somewhat different. In my opinion, birds should not be subjected to the stresses of exhibition during the demanding period of moulting or producing new breeding plumage. The trauma of being suddenly subjected to dramatic changes of temperature, light-hours and crowd-proximity can result in a suspension of the physiological process for an indeterminate period. In fanciers' parlance, the bird becomes 'stuck in the moult' with the result that the new set of plumage is not fully developed and the bird is generally useless for exhibition purposes for the rest of that show season. For this reason any bird which has only partially completed its post-breeding seasonal moult or is in the process of developing breeding plumage should not be exhibited.

Some judges may argue that, in the case of many of these species, it is not possible to confirm that a true pair is being shown when a male in eclipse plumage is partnered with a female in virtually identical garb. However, as there are literally hundreds of exotic species which are not sexually dimorphic and which must be accepted as 'pairs' on the show bench in good faith, this objection is untenable.

It could also be argued that it is very difficult for anyone, except a very knowledgeable specialist, to identify the various species of Weavers and Whydahs when they are in eclipse plumage. Again, this is not acceptable as a valid argument as the question of the rarity of the species is not a particularly important one when assessing the merits of any birds. As the rarer Weavers and Whydahs are, in the main, just as easy to keep as their commoner relatives, the question of rarity is even less important in the case of this group of species.

5.4 **A fine male Paradise Whydah** (*Steganura paradisaea*) in full breeding plumage. The long-tailed Whydahs often do well on the show bench when staged in fine condition.

CHAPTER 6

Show Cages

PROVISION OF SUITABLE CAGES

At many *small* livestock shows in this country, the show cages or pens for the exhibits are provided by the society which organises the show, a procedure which is also followed in the case of competitive cage bird exhibitions elsewhere in Europe. In Britain however, the exhibitor of exotic species, and other varieties of cage birds, must provide his own show cages.

As has already been stated there are virtually no rules or *standards* which apply nationally to the pastime of foreign bird exhibiting, and this is equally true in the matter of show cages. There is therefore no requirement, as there is with other varieties, to exhibit foreign species in standard show cages because these simply do not exist. Practically all show schedules, however, state that, where no standard show cage exists, **birds must be shown in a cage suitable for the species**.

The essential requirements of the show cage are that it should show the bird to the best advantage, allowing the judge a clear, close-range view of the exhibit while, at the same time, permitting the bird to stretch its wings fully and indulge in a reasonable amount of activity. Over the years, certain designs of show cages have become generally accepted as being the most suitable for particular genera or groups of exotic species. Although these are in common use, there are also to be seen at shows a wide variety of home produced show cages of varying degrees of suitability and workmanship. Many such cages are, of course, well made and of good design, but some leave much to be desired, and it is probably best to purchase suitable cages unless one is reasonably skilful with carpentry tools. Professionally-made show cages are by no means cheap to buy, however, and as the 'do-it-yourself' enthusiast may wish to make his own, or perhaps arrange for a more skilled acquaintance to make some for him, a detailed description of the various designs suitable for foreign species may be useful.

CAGE DESIGN

Basically, all Foreign Bird show cages are of box-type construction with wire fronts, except for those used to exhibit the larger Parrot-like birds. In the latter case, these species are normally shown in the domestic-type cage of heavy-gauge all-metal construction. All cages must be of sound construction to prevent the possible escape of the inmates and also to stand up to any vigorous handling which they may receive in transit. It is also desirable, of course, that the show cages should be as light as possible, to facilitate handling and to diminish the costs of rail transport which are calculated by the weight of the consignment.

Material

Plywood is probably the most frequently used material for show cage construction as it complies with most of the essential requirements and is easily obtainable. It does have one disadvantage, however, in that the layers of veneer forming the plywood are liable to separate in wet conditions. As a result of the spillage of drinking water and the frequent need for thorough washing, show cages do tend to receive regular exposure to dampness. It is consequently preferable to use marine ply for cage construction, particularly if less costly off-cuts are available, as it will resist deterioration of this nature much better than ordinary plywood.

Cage Fronts

The wire cage fronts may be purchased ready-made in which case, of course, the dimensions of the cage must be designed to accommodate the front. Alternatively, suitable tinned wire and punch bars can also be obtained from appliance suppliers, and any size of cage front can be made to the desired specification. Although this latter method is less costly and allows wider scope in design, it is more time consuming and requires a greater degree of skill. An important consideration, whether purchasing or making a show cage front, is the spacing between the vertical wire bars. Standard manufacturers' fronts are usually available in two spacings, ½ inch (1.3cm) and ³/₈ inch (1cm). Bars which are spaced at

6.1 **Poorly exhibited bird**. This show cage is much too small for the exhibit — **a Diamond Dove** — with the result that the bird's tail is constantly being crushed against the side of the cage. The tail feathers will inevitably become frayed and broken, ruining the exhibit's chances of getting into the cards. Note also the loose wire in the bottom left corner of the cage front — a Waxbill-sized exhibit could easily escape through this gap.

½ inch intervals will contain virtually all foreign species, *provided* that they are not bent or distorted in any way. If, however, they are even slightly bent — and this could occur almost unnoticed — some of the smaller species, such as Gold-breasted Waxbills, could escape. It is advisable, therefore, to use fronts with ³/₈ inch (1 cm) spacing between the bars for all species up to, say the size of the Red-eared Waxbill and ½ inch spacing for species larger than this.

Perching Arrangement

A very important feature in the design of any show cage, and one which frequently receives little attention from some exhibitors, is the perching arrangement. If a bird is unable to perch naturally and comfortably, it cannot show itself to advantage and is unlikely to achieve its full potential as an exhibit.

On occasion, Foreign Bird exhibitors may use the standard

6.2 **Show Cage suitable for a pair of small seedeaters**, such as Silverbills or Waxbills. Note opening of drinker in front rail for easy and safe watering by stewards at shows. Seedeaters' show cages must never be decorated — only a seed floor covering (as shown in the photograph) is necessary.

Budgerigar or Zebra Finch show cages for some of their exhibits, and although these are perfectly suitable for some species, the perches may need to be replaced in some instances. The standard Budgerigar perch is generally unsuitable for most of the exotic species which can be adequately shown in a Budgerigar show cage, and Zebra Finch size perches will probably have to be provided. For the smaller Waxbills, however, even these latter perches will be of too great a diameter and the slimmer purpose-made size will have to be used. The recommended diameters of the different sizes of perches suitable for the various show cages will be found later in this chapter, on the pages dealing with the dimensions of the cages.

In some cases, of course, the rigid round dowel-type of perch may not be the most suitable for the species in question, and a more natural material may be utilised. The small Nectar-feeders, such as the Sunbirds for example, will fare better if thin cane is artistically used to provide the perching facilities, and the larger Softbills can be provided with natural twigs and branches. The perches must, of course, be simple in design, free from sharp projections and must not restrict or impede the movements of the birds.

Generally, the arrangement of the perches, whether dowel or natural, should induce the bird to display its profile to the judge. In other words, the line of the perches will be roughly at right angles to the rear wall of the show cage. The judge can then persuade the bird to face either end of the cage, so that he can examine the whole of the bird adequately. Most show cages supplied by the trade are fitted with perches in this position, with the exception of those for Parrot-like birds, both Lovebirds and the larger species. In these instances the show cages are usually fitted with a single perch, which is fixed laterally and runs parallel with the rear wall of the cage. Although this arrangement may have some advantage, it has one major drawback from the judge's point of view, in that it is virtually impossible to see the back of the birds clearly. Invariably Parrot-like species will sit facing the front of the show cage on this type of perch and it is an almost hopeless task trying to get them to turn their backs to the judge. As a full rear view of the birds is impossible, the judge must attempt to examine the backs and wings of the birds by peering down from the top of the cage. It would certainly be advantageous if the perches in the show cages of Parrot-like species were to be fixed to the rear of the cage as with other species.

It will be noted that perches of the dowel type fitted to the rear of the cages are generally attached to a circular wooden rose, which acts as an anti-leverage device against the weight or impact of the bird on the perch. It is essential to ensure before each show that all perches, of any type, are securely screwed to the cage as it will probably ruin an exhibit's chances of winning if its perches have become loosened or detached.

Drinkers and Food Receptacles

All show cages must, of course, be fitted with drinkers and, in some instances, food receptacles as well. The plastic inverted fountain-type of drinker, which can be fixed to a clip attached to the wire bars of the cage front, may be used on the larger size of show cage where it is not likely to obscure the judge's view of the

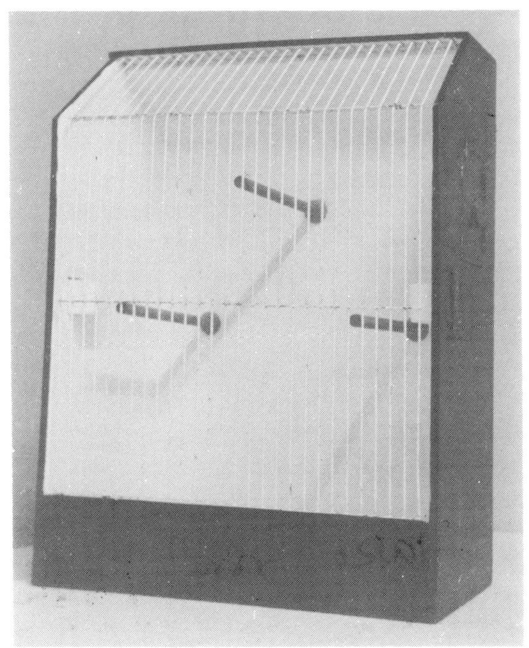

6.3 **Typical Whydah Show Cage**. Specifically-designed for exhibiting the long–tailed species of Whydahs. The perches are positioned well above the level of the floor to prevent the birds' long tails becoming frayed or soiled; the drinking receptacles are positioned at perch level for similar reasons. The cage front is angled at the top to allow ample light to fall on the exhibit and to afford the judge a good all-round view of the birds.

birds. It is not very suitable, however, for the relatively small Seedeater show cage, and for these cages, the most commonly-used type is the square-shaped open drinker fixed to the back of a small access door cut in the front rail. This type of drinker is usually slotted into a metal holder so that it can be easily removed for cleaning, and the metal should be aluminium or other non-ferric to prevent the rusting which would otherwise be inevitable due to the wet conditions.

Food receptacles are not normally required in Seedeaters' cages as the food supply is used as a floor covering in this case. Softbills' cages on the other hand will have to be fitted with containers for soft food, fruit or mealworms as appropriate. These too should be securely fixed to prevent spillage but should be capable of easy removal for cleaning. The inverted fountain-type of drinker is also often used as a container for supplying nectar mixtures to Sugarbirds and similar species. As water and nectar, and possibly other food, will probably have to be renewed by the stewards during the show, it is advisable that access to all drinkers and food containers can be had from outside the cage without the necessity of opening the door. Where drinkers and food receptacles are fitted to the inside of small doors cut into the front rail as previously mentioned, they must be provided with 'escape wires', which effectively close the opening when the receptacle is removed for re-filling.

Cage Colours

Finally there is the question of which colours may be used for painting the show cage, and here again we rely on tradition rather than regulation. Almost invariably the interiors of Foreign Birds show cages are white and the exteriors are black. There is little doubt that a white interior is probably the most suitable colour for showing the majority of exotic species to advantage. In the case of predominantly white birds, however, a white cage background is not the most satisfactory from the judge's viewpoint. Fortunately there are not very many foreign species which appear on the show bench which are mainly white, but the White Java Sparrow and Rothschild's Grackle are two cases in point. It seems apparent that such species would be seen to much better advantage if the interior of their show cages were to be painted light blue, as is used on the inside of New Colour Canary show cages, for example.

Some may argue that a Foreign Bird show cage with a blue interior would constitute a 'marked cage', but as there is no such thing as a standard cage for exotic species, there can be no 'marked cage' in terms of a deviation from the standard. The theory behind the 'marked cage' objection, of course, is that an exhibitor must have nothing abnormal about his show cages, which would reveal his identity to the judge and thereby give him an unfair advantage in the competition. This has always appeared to me to be rather a weak argument, as it would be far simpler for the dishonest fancier to notify the judge of the numbers on his cage labels before the show, in the extremely unlikely event of both parties being intent on any underhand conspiracy. There can, therefore, be no objection to the use of show cages with blue interiors for showing species with predominantly white plumage, although it is most unusual to find this practice being applied.

With regard to the actual paints, a black gloss finish is most suitable for the outside of the cages, but it is preferable to use a brilliant white vinyl silk emulsion on the interiors. This is easily cleaned and reduces the reflected glare which can occur if white gloss is used.

The wire front of the show cage must also be painted, of course, and opinion is divided as to whether black or white is the most suitable colour. A wire front painted black seems to interfere least with vision when focussing on the birds behind it, and therefore this seems to be the best colour to use.

Carrying Cases

When show cages are to be conveyed to a distant show by rail transport, or certain other means, they must be enclosed in a suitable case. These 'carrying cases', as they are known, must satisfy similar requirements to the show cages themselves, in that they must be of sound design and construction and as light in weight as possible in order to minimise freight charges. Where show cages for small Seedeaters are concerned, the carrying case may be designed to hold either two or four cages of similar dimensions, depending on the requirements of the exhibitor. Large show cages, such as those used for most Softbills and the larger Parrot-like species, will normally require a carrying case for each individual cage.

Irrespective of size, however, the carrying case must be designed and constructed so that the show cages fit easily, but snugly, inside in such a way that they cannot sway and bump around during transit. On those occasions when it may prove necessary to convey, for example, three show cages in a carrying case which is designed to contain four, the resulting unwanted space in the case must be filled by using a cardboard box of suitable size, or an empty show cage (with the front removed so that the stewards, when unpacking, can clearly see that it is a 'blank').

The carrying case must also be provided with means of ventilation and a suitable number of holes can be cut or drilled in the sides of the case. Where the ventilation holes are of greater diameter than 3/8 inch (1cm) they should be covered with wire gauze to eliminate the risk of rodents gaining access to the attractive supplies of foodstuff within. Ventilation holes must not be situated on the top surface of the carrying case, as they are then liable to be

6.4 **Carrying Case**: useful when transporting a number of show cages. It is essential when sending exhibits by rail. The show cages must fit neatly inside so that they cannot be overturned during transit. Note the ventilation holes in the ends of carrying case.

obstructed by other cases or packages being stacked on top during transit.

If a strong and secure handle is fixed to the lid of the carrying case, this will not only facilitate handling, but will also encourage those involved to keep the case the right way up. When being conveyed by public transport, a label, inscribed 'Live Birds — Will Die if Delayed' should be fixed to the lid of the carrying case, in addition to the destination address label.

Designs and Dimensions for Specific Varieties

In the following pages are suggested some designs and dimensions of show cages suitable for various categories of foreign birds.

Plate 3 Foreign Birds

Plate 4 Foreign Birds

In those instances where an exhibitor may wish to show a particular species and is unsure of the correct show cage to use (or does not own one of the recommended design), he should err on the side of generosity and utilise a cage which is larger than may be necessary, rather than one which is in any way too restricted.

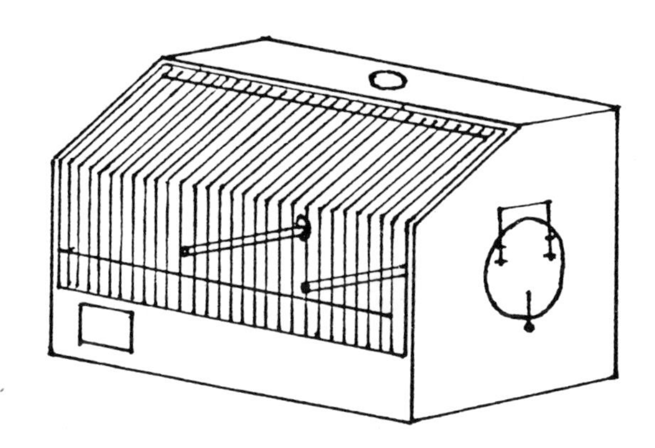

6.5 **Show Cage I**

Small Seedeaters (e.g. Waxbills, Munias, Siskins, etc.)
Cage dimensions — 14 inches (35.6cm) long × 8 inches wide (20.3cm) wide × 10 inches (25.4cm)
Spacing between bars — 3/8 inch (1cm) (Waxbills and smaller Munias) ½ inch (1.3cm) (others)
Perch Diameter — 8 mm (smaller species) 10 mm (others)

Larger Seedeaters (e.g. Long-tailed Grassfinches, Java Sparrows, etc.)
Cage Dimensions — 18 inches (45.7cm) long × 8 inches (20.3cm) wide × 12 inches (30.5cm) high
Spacing between bars — ½ inch (1.3cm)
Perch Diameter — 12 mm

Large Seedeaters (e.g. Cardinals, Hawfinches, Grosbeaks, etc.)
Cage Dimensions — 20 inches (50.8) long × 10 inches (25.4cm) wide × 15 inches high (38cm).
Spacing between bars — ½ inch (1.3cm)
Perch Diameter — 15 mm

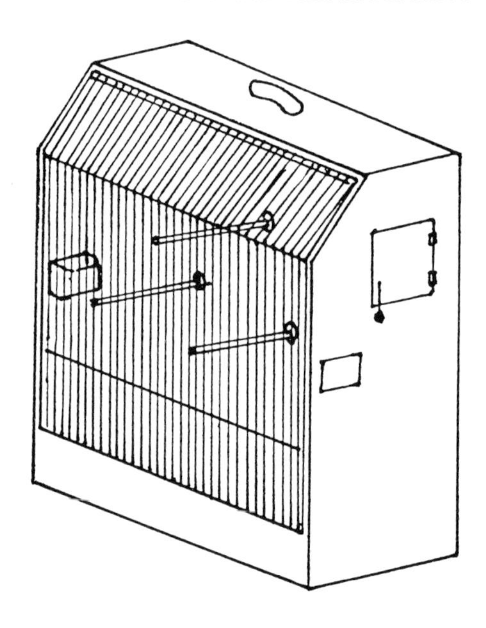

6.6 **Show Cage II**

Whydahs

Cage dimensions — 15 inches (38cm) long × 9 inches (22.8cm) wide × 20 inches (50.8cm) high

Spacing between bars — ½ inch (1.3cm)

Perch Diameter — 10–12 mm (according to species)

Note: Drinking receptacles are postitioned approx 9 inches (22.8cm) above floor level with perches affording ready access.

Parrakeets and Lorikeets (including all long-tailed Psittacines)

Cage Dimensions — The cage described above for Whydahs may be used satisfactorily for the smaller parrakeets (Turquoisines, Red-bellied Conures, etc.) provided that the topmost perch is removed.

For larger species (e.g. Ringnecks, Broadtails, etc.) the dimensions should be increased to: 24 inches (61cm) long × 12 inches (30.5cm) wide × 24 inches (61cm) high.

Perch Diameters — 15 mm (Grass Parrakeets and similar) 22 mm (Ringnecks, etc.)

Note: The cage recommended for the larger parrakeets may also be used for exhibiting the typical short-tailed Parrots. Alternatively, the all-metal domestic parrot cage may be used, which is less susceptible to damage, particularly where Cockatoos are being shown.

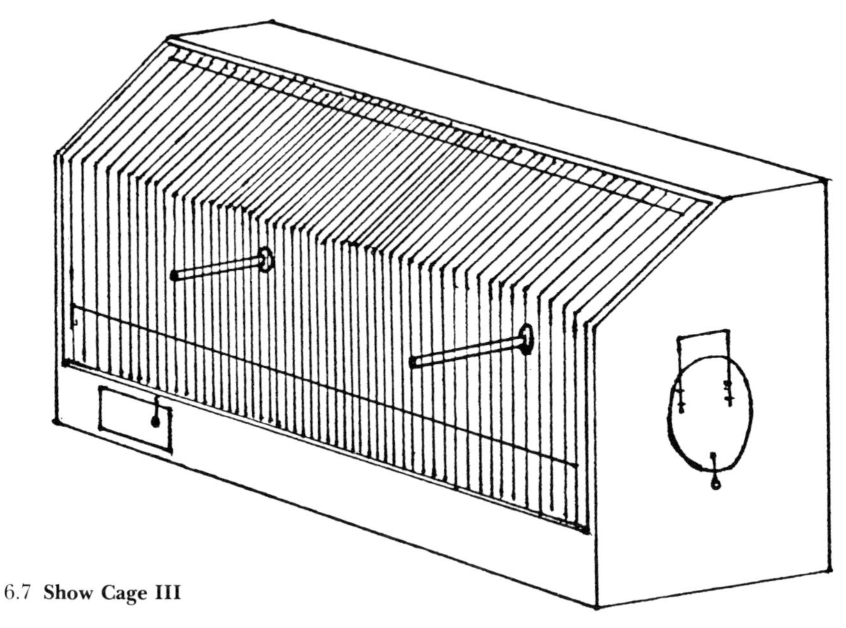

6.7 **Show Cage III**

Small Softbills (e.g. Hummingbirds, Flowerpeckers, etc.)
Cage Dimensions — 24 inches (61cm) long × 12 inches (30.5cm) wide × 20 inches (50.8cm) high
Spacing between bars — $^3/_8$ inch (1cm)
Perch Diameter — 3–5 mm according to species (cane or natural twig)

Medium Softbills (e.g. Thrushes, Bulbuls, Tanagers, etc.)
Cage Dimensions — 24 inches (61cm) long × 10 inches (25.4cm) wide × 16 inches (40.6cm) high
Spacing between bars — $\frac{1}{2}$ inch (1.3cm)
Perch Diameter — 12–15 mm according to species (dowel or natural twig)

Large Softbills (e.g. Jays, Laughing Thrushes, Touracos, etc.)
Cage Dimensions — 36 inches (91.4cm) long × 24 inches (61cm) wide × 30 inches (76.2cm) high
Spacing between bars — $\frac{1}{2}$ inch (1.3cm) to $\frac{3}{4}$ inch (1.9cm)
Perch Diameter — 22–35 mm (according to species)

Chapter 7

Show Preparation

INITIAL EXAMINATION OF STOCK

As the breeding season draws to a close and the first show announcements begin to appear in *Cage and Aviary Birds*, the thoughts of the fancier will turn to the prospect of exhibiting some of his stock. His first task will be to examine his birds, including any youngsters he may have bred, in order to select his show team for the season.

It is not only new additions to the fancier's stock, which require careful examination, but also birds which may have done well on the show bench during the previous show season. During the course of the breeding season such birds will probably have been housed in outdoor flights, and physical damage from a variety of sources may have occurred. Attacks by cats or owls can result in lost limbs or more minor mutilation; aggressive species housed in adjoining flights (particularly in the case of Parrot-like birds) may amputate their neighbours' toes; night frights may cause panic producing injuries by abrasion against the wire-netting; or the odd toe-nail may become entangled in nesting material and be pulled out. Although most of such injuries are of a fairly minor nature and will not affect the bird's potential in the breeding aviary, they render the individual quite useless as an exhibition specimen. It is, therefore, essential that the fancier should identify any birds which have sustained damage in this way and discard them from his show team at the commencement of the show season.

Damage to plumage during nesting is, of course, almost inevitable, but this will be rectified by the moult and the growth of new feathers when the breeding season is over.

TRAINING

Birds which are physically sound must then receive a certain amount of training if they are to achieve the steadiness which is desirable in a good show specimen. It is quite hopeless to expect a bird taken straight from a large outdoor aviary, or dealer's establishment, to accept the restricted confines of a small show cage without showing some signs of panic.

The champion Canary or Budgerigar exhibitor will train his birds to an exceptional degree of steadiness, but, fortunately, those who exhibit Foreign species are not normally required to install such a high standard of discipline into their birds. The judge must, however, be given a reasonable opportunity to study each exhibit in some detail, and it is difficult enough trying to spot missing claws on the tiny feet of a normally active pair of Waxbills, for example, without the added complication of the birds being completely untrained and frightened.

Some species will require more show cage experience than others, for example, the Weaver group which are, on the whole, quite unsteady, as mentioned earlier. However, the basic training requirements for all species are virtually the same.

Firstly, the potential show specimen must become accustomed to the relatively limited confines of the show cage in which it will be exhibited. If the layout of the birdroom allows, an old show cage can be fitted in a semi-permanent position on the end of the stock or flight cages with access between. The birds may then be encouraged into the show cage, without alarm, and a sliding door or shutter can be used to confine them in the show cage for the desired length of time. If a suitable titbit, such as a piece of spray millet or favourite fruit, is fed to the bird each time it is restricted to the show cage, it may even come to regard the experience as pleasurable.

It is very probable that many fanciers will be unable to set up training show cages in the manner just described, because of the physical limitations of their existing cage lay-outs. In these cases it will generally be necessary for the birds to be caught up by hand and placed in individual show cages. The catching-up of the birds should be carried out as quickly and efficiently as possible, without fluster, and great care must be taken to avoid damage to the plumage in the process.

Where completely untrained birds are placed in a show cage for the first time, they may dash against the bars of the front or crouch on the floor. At this stage, the fancier should make no attempt to get them to perch properly, but should keep well away from the show cage to allow the birds to become accustomed to the new environment. If undisturbed they will soon settle down and eventually find their way onto the perches. When the birds are using the perches freely and regularly, the fancier should approach the show cage slowly and quietly (but not furtively!) which will probably result in the inmates repeating their fluttering or crouching act. An unflustered, tactical withdrawal by the fancier will allow the birds to settle down again. The approach and retreat tactics should be repeated indefinitely until the birds permit the fancier to approach without signs of panic.

When this stage has been reached the fancier should then spend as much time as possible in close proximity to the caged birds while he is working or relaxing in the birdroom. As the birds become more and more steady, it is advisable to subject them to as many new experiences as possible, such as blowing one's nose as flamboyantly as possible, whistling and talking loudly — it does not really matter if your neighbours think you are slightly mad! It is also a useful idea, when visiting the birdroom, to wear unusually bright or light-coloured clothing occasionally, if one does not normally do so. It is quite amazing how many birds will react in an alarmed manner, if their owner enters the birdroom wearing a rarely-worn cap or light raincoat to which they are not accustomed. As they are likely to encounter all shapes and colours of dress when being exhibited at shows, the birds should receive as much pre-show experience in this matter as possible.

Visitors to the birdroom should also be encouraged — after the end of the breeding season, preferably — in order to allow show stock to become accustomed to seeing the human form in the plural. It may also be thought desirable, on occasions, to bring the

---

7.1 **Yellow Sparrow** (*Auripasser luteus*)
A prettily-marked species sometimes advertised by dealers as the Golden Song Sparrow. Its song is not particularly notable but it is a hardy species and suitable for the beginner in some respects. However, it is not easy to breed, and tends to be rather unsteady which considerably lessens its value as an exhibit. It is found in varoius subspecific races from East Africa across to Southern Arabia.

show cages indoors to a busy part of the household, provided that care is taken to protect the birds from any four-footed domestic pets or very young children.

The actual amount of time required to train any bird will vary according to the species and the temperament of the individual bird, but a considerable number of hours, spread over several days, will be necessary. When the birds have achieved a reasonable degree of steadiness, they should be entered at the local society's Table Show or Members' Show, which are often fairly small events but extremely useful for 'breaking-in' both the birds and their owners.

SELECTION AND MAINTENANCE OF BIRDS IN SHOW CONDITION

When selecting his entries for a particular show, the fancier must decide whether he is going to show his birds as pairs or as singles. Although I have seen one show schedule where the Foreign Bird classification was divided into classes for pairs, and a corresponding number of classes for single birds, it is generally accepted that either pairs or singles may be entered in any of the classes in the Foreign section. It is also a general rule, however, that it is preferable to show small seedeaters in pairs, and large species such as Touracos, or aggressive species such as Humming birds, as singles. Incidentally, Humming birds may be shown as pairs, if desired, but it is usually advisable to sub-divide the show cage by means of a fine wire or perspex partition to prevent fighting between male and female.

Pairing

It is essential when showing pairs of any species that they be properly matched. Rather than exhibit a first class male with a mediocre female, or vice versa, it is preferable to discard the individual which does not come up to the desired standard, and show the superior specimen as a single. When selecting pairs they must be evenly matched for size, colour and plumage pattern where appropriate, and one should take care not to form pairs of different sub-species or geographical races, which may be of similar, but not identical, appearance. It is also possible that, even where one has a perfectly-matched pair, one of the birds may break

7.2 **Badly-matched pair of Red-Eared Waxbills**. The bird on the left is a fine specimen in perfect plumage but it has been matched with an inferior partner. The Red-ear on the right has several feathers missing from its tail and the feathering above the beak is also imperfect. The exhibitor would be advised to show the superior specimen as a single exhibit and leave the other bird at home.

its tail, or drop a couple of flight feathers, prior to the show. In these circumstances, too, the defective partner should be left in the birdroom and the perfect specimen shown by itself.

Plumage

If a bird accidentally damages its tail or flight feathers, they will not be replaced until the broken 'stumps' have been removed. This will generally happen at the annual moult, by natural shedding of the damaged plumage, but if a favoured show specimen sustains broken feathers during the early part of the show season, the fancier can accelerate the process by pulling out the 'stump'. The larger feathers, such as flights and tail, will take approximately six to eight weeks to regenerate, while smaller ones will be replaced in a much shorter period. I must emphasise that the removal of defective plumage is advocated only to allow new feathers to commence growth and the bird should not be shown until the new feathers have been completely formed.

Malpractices

It is not considered fair play — and is often contrary to the show rules — to exhibit a bird whose plumage has been drawn, clipped, dyed, or otherwise manipulated in order to mislead or deceive the judge. There are, in any event, few circumstances, where the 'treatment' of plumage in this way would benefit the exhibitor of foreign species, and fanciers would be well advised to refrain from any such attempts at deception.

Bathing Facilities

The condition of a bird's plumage governs its ability to fly and escape from danger, and is, therefore, one of its most important attributes. Given a reasonable chance, all birds will endeavour to keep their plumage in as near perfect condition as possible, but in confinement a little assistance from the fancier is desirable. The least he can do is to provide adequate bathing facilities, and shallow water receptacles, of adequate size for the species in question, should be constantly available in cages and flights. The majority of species will make regular and frequent use of this facility in order to keep their plumage in sparkling condition, although a few prefer to cavort amongst soaked grasses or wet foliage as a method of bathing. Fine sand dust baths should be provided for Quail and other species which enjoy this form of personal hygiene.

Cage Conditions

There is little point, however, in providing bathing facilities if the birds are kept in dirty conditions and it is essential that the interiors of all cages and flights are maintained in a clean condition. This is particularly important in the case of accommodation housing exhibition stock, and special attention should be given to the cleanliness of perches and floors to prevent foot troubles as well as soiling of plumage. Apart from regular cleaning and renewal or scrubbing of perches, one should take care to avoid overcrowding the birds as this will inevitably lead to plumage damage of one sort or another.

Softbills — especially those being fed on nectar mixtures and soft fruits — will require far more frequent attention than the seedeat-

7.3 **European Waxwing** (*Bombycilla garrulus*) a bird of fine plumage – soft vinaceous brown feathering. The American Cedar Waxwing (*Bombycilla cedrorum*) is imported from time to time and is of very similar appearance.

ers, as their perches are inclined to become very sticky as a result of beak-wiping, and their copious, liquid droppings quickly foul the interior of their accommodation.

Newspapers prove a good floor covering in cages and indoor flights, although, some birds tend to nibble at the paper or tear it into strips — Java Sparrows are quite prone to this pastime — and those with white plumage become rather grubby through coming into contact with the newsprint. It is advisable, during the show season, to replace the newspaper floor coverings with a more suitable material, such as sand, for example, which will not adversely affect those species with white or pale plumage.

Grooming

Although experienced Canary fanciers sometimes hand-wash their birds prior to showing, it is generally unnecessary for the foreign bird exhibitor to indulge in this practice. It should certainly

7.4 **A useful fine-mist handspray** for spraying exhibits. Not all exotic species will require such pre-show treatment, but it is advantageous for some parrot-like and certain other species which do not bathe in the usual manner.

never be undertaken by the inexperienced, but if it is ever considered to be absolutely necessary, one should endeavour to obtain a practical demonstration from a local Canary fancier with first-hand knowledge.

It may, however, be found desirable to spray show specimens to add that extra lustre to the plumage. A one pint ($\frac{1}{2}$ litre) capacity horticultural spray, capable of producing a fine mist, will be found adequate and the birds to be sprayed can be placed in an old show cage or a suitable all-wire cage. The birds should receive a good soaking and must then be accommodated in a warm, draught-free environment to dry off. Spraying once or twice in the week before the show will be adequate, but this should not be done less than two days before the actual day of the show. Clean, lukewarm water is perfectly satisfactory for spraying, but it is possible to obtain proprietary additives which are designed to give an added sheen to the feathers. These are obtainable from many pet shops and dealers' establishments, if required.

Show Cage

In addition to ensuring that the birds are well-groomed in preparation for the show, one should ascertain that the show cages which the birds are to occupy are in equally faultless condition. It is, of course, the bird itself which has been entered for evaluation by the judge, but the manner in which it is staged by the exhibitor must also be taken into account. Where a bird has been entered in a show cage which is filthy, unsuitable with regard to size or diameter of perches or otherwise in unsatisfactory condition, this will undoubtedly detract from the merits of the exhibit and, in strong competition, could mean the difference between first and second places.

When a bird, or pair of birds, have been confined to the relatively limited area of a show cage for two to three days, the perches and the interior of the cage will inevitably become fouled by droppings. After each show, therefore, the show cages should be thoroughly cleaned out, and the perches and interior scrubbed with hot water and detergent. The exterior should also be washed clean and the cage labels, and any award labels which may have been allocated at the show, must be removed from the front bottom rail of the cages.

This procedure should also be carried out at the end of each show season — dirty cages which have lain unattended all summer are quite difficult to clean. Before storing the cleaned show cages away in their carrying cases, or before the start of the following show season, the cages should be repainted if the paintwork is in any way defective. Any painting which is required should be carried out well before the date of the first show, and I can personally vouch for the fact that the judge's temper will not be improved by having his fingers smeared with black gloss paint which has failed to dry. There is also the risk, of course, that a freshly painted cage, used too soon, could ruin the birds' plumage.

It is also a good idea to examine closely the wire show cage fronts together with the catches on the drinkers and cage doors, at the start of each show season. It is not uncommon, particularly with cages that have been subjected to a great deal of usage, for the vertical wires to become loosened from the holes in the horizontal punch bar. In such instances, a neat and delicate re-soldering operation will be necessary to restore the security of the show cage, as it is only too easy for the smaller birds to escape if only a single wire is out of position.

The catches on many show cage drinkers are often made of thin wire, although the brass catch of the type used on standard Zebra Finch show cages seem much more durable, and less likely to become snagged on clothing, for example. With regular use the thin wire catches on the drinkers and cage door become weakened — particularly if they are a little stiff to operate — and break off. These must, of course, be renewed before the show cage is used again, in order to prevent the accidental opening of the drinkers and possible escapes.

DECORATION OF THE SHOW CAGE

Having now ensured that the birds and the show cages are in perfect condition for showing, the exhibitor must consider one final matter before bringing together the two parts of his exhibit—the decoration of the cage. There is a great temptation for beginners to try and convert the interior of their show cages into miniature replicas of Kew Gardens, and, while such an arrangement might form an attractive display unit in a lounge, on the show bench the end result is usually that the birds cannot be seen to full advantage by the judge. It is very frustrating for the latter to try and examine small species if they are constantly hopping in and out of dangling foliage.

As with almost every other aspect of foreign bird exhibiting, there are no official rules governing the decoration of show cages. It is, however, the generally accepted practice that the cages of seedeaters should not be decorated in any way whatsoever, with the sole exception of the various species of Quail, which spend the whole of their time on the cage floor. The only addition to the show cages of any other species of seedeater should be the floor covering, which generally comprises of seed only. Pannicum millet is favoured for the cages of Waxbills and other small species, but some of the larger millets, such as plate, may be used, with or without the addition of canary seed in the case of the larger species.

A canary/millet mixture is also suitable for the smaller Parrot-like birds, such as the Grass Parrakeets, but the cage floors of the larger species are generally covered with sunflower seed. A floor covering, comprising of seed in this way, serves two purposes; it provides a neat finish to the bottom of the cage, effectively masking the untidy fouling by droppings which would otherwise be more apparent, and it also supplies the inmates of the cage with their source of food for the duration of the show.

For both these reasons, the exhibitor should not try and economise too much on this aspect of show preparation. A liberal quantity of seed should be spread evenly over the cage floor to a depth of about ½ inch, in the case of the millets and other smaller seeds, and rather more in the case of sunflower. These approximate quantities should adequately supply the food requirements of the birds for the two days' duration of the average show.

Incidentally, it will be apparent that birds, which have just returned from a show, will be eager to satisfy their need for grit, and the exhibitor should ensure that the grit pots are topped up with both soluble (calcium) and insoluble grit on their return.

In the case of **Quail show cages**, on the other hand, a certain amount of herbaceous decor is permissible. The layout should be simple, uncluttered and unobstructive, with moss being probably the most suitable floor covering. A modest arrangement of grasses or ferns securely fixed to the rear wall of the cage will enhance the final effect, if tastefully done. It should perhaps be pointed out at this stage that cage decoration is rather like flower arrangement; some people, who appear to be naturally gifted, are very good at it; others can produce an acceptable, if uninspired, effort; the rest can only achieve a result which is totally devoid of merit. If an exhibitor should fall into this last category, he would be well advised to ignore completely the question of cage decoration, and allow his birds to establish their own merits in a clean, bright, uncluttered show cage.

The decoration of **Softbill** show cages is, however, accepted practice in the case of species up to about large Tanager-size. Here again, it is essential that the decoration must not be overdone, even in the larger cages normally used for Humming birds and Sunbirds. A single bloom, such as a carnation of a suitable pastel shade, fixed neatly in a test-tube type of container in a corner of the cage, with perhaps, a small spray of fern will generally be adequate. It is a mistake to try and re-create a 'natural' jungle-like setting on the show bench, however desirable such conditions may be in the breeding accommodation.

Where the single bloom form of decor is used, it will be found that the most suitable form of floor covering is thick, white blotting paper, which will absorb the rather liquid droppings of nectar-feeders and other small softbills. If a slightly more elaborate setting

7.5 **Softbill Show Cage** — should be decorated with discretion. The neat floral spray in the corner does not detract from this pair of **Pekin Robins** (*Leiothrix lutea*) but one sometimes sees exhibits completely overshadowed, or even partially obscured, by attempts to 'enhance' the birds' background.

is planned, and this would perhaps be justified in the case of species such as the White-capped Redstart, then moss would probably be a more suitable material for the purpose.

The setting which one is trying to achieve must largely reflect the natural habitat of the species being exhibited, in such a way that the bird is able to move around its show cage in a perfectly normal manner. The word 'reflect' rather than 'reproduce' has been used deliberately, and no apology is made for stressing again that the show cage must not be cluttered up with various contents of the exhibitor's shrubbery and flower borders.

Quail (and Quail Finches) must be allowed to walk around on the floors of their cages; Humming birds must be permitted to hover in front of their nectar bottles; Finches and other perching birds must be supplied with suitable perches, and so on. An excellent example of the point in question, was an Indian Sandpiper, which was to be seen exhibited at the **National Exhibition of Cage and**

Aviary Birds a number of years ago. This is a rather unusual species to encounter on the show bench, but the show cage was perfectly decorated with a little sea sand, a few pebbles and seashells, to indicate a typical natural habitat for the species.

Similarly, if it is proposed to exhibit any of the Woodpeckers or Nuthatches, it will be necessary to provide a rough, vertical surface to which they can cling naturally. This can be done by fixing natural bark or a suitable cork reconstruction to the rear of the cage, but this must be as secure as possible as it would be quite disastrous, as far as the exhibit's chances of success were concerned, if the bark lining should become detached prior to judging.

Although it is common practice to decorate the show cages of small Softbills, this is not a practical proposition in the case of the larger species. Any decoration in the show cages of birds as large as Touracos or Tree Pies, for example, is liable to become disarrayed either by accident or design on the part of the occupants. Thick blotting paper may be used as floor covering for cages to be occupied by the medium-sized species such as Bulbuls, and wood-shavings are often used in the cages of the larger birds. Sawdust is not a very satisfactory material for floor covering as it invariably gets blown about by the wing movements of the birds, and has a tendency to choke up the food and water containers.

In the case of the larger species, some exhibitors have fitted 'false' slatted floors to their show cages so that the copious droppings produced by such birds fall through the slats into the bottom of the cage, which is suitably covered. In this way the bird's feet and plumage are less likely to become soiled by contact with the droppings.

Other than in the case of the seedeaters, all food — and of course, water — must be supplied in suitable receptacles and care must be taken to ensure that these are not hidden or obstructed by the materials used to decorate the cage. Food containers must be of sufficient size to hold a reasonable quantity of food, and should be securely located in such a way that they cannot be tipped over. It is often impractical to provide sufficient food for Softbills for the duration of the show prior to their despatch, and the normal practice in such cases is to bring (or send) the necessary food in ample quantities in suitable containers, clearly marked with the class and cage number of the exhibit, together with any special instructions. The stewards at the show will then be responsible for

1A
2
3
1
4
5

feeding the birds in the required manner. It is, of course, unnecessary to fill the drinkers in the show cages before sending the birds to the show, as the stewards must also ensure that drinking water is available to all the exhibits for the duration of the event.

In all cases where stewards will have the task of replenishing food and water supplies, it is essential that the appropriate receptacles are so situated that they can be refilled without the need to open the cage door. If the steward is obliged to open the cage in order to reach the receptacles, the exhibitor will have little grounds for complaint if his bird escapes.

7.6 **South American** *Sporophila*: care must be taken with all perching birds to supply suitable show cage arrangements.

1,1A Guttural Finch (*Sporophila nigricollis*) male and female
2. Lined Finch (*S. americana*)
3. Reddish Finch (*S. nigroaurantia*)
4. White-throated Finch (*S. albigularis*)
5. Bluish Finch (*S. caerulescens*)

(*Sporophila* — fairly large genus of about 60 South American species. A few are imported into this country in small numbers from time to time. Although lacking bright colours they are, on the whole, attractively marked and deserve more attention. Not a difficult species to keep but true pairs may sometimes be difficult to obtain. Unfortunately, they must compete in the Rare Seedeater section where competition is often formidable.)

CHAPTER 8

Mechanics of Showing

Many potential exhibitors are apprehensive of the seeming complexities of entering and staging their birds at an open show. Not only are they sometimes confused by the paperwork and the significance of patronage nominations, but they are, initially, wary of leaving their cherished birds to the tender mercies of complete strangers for a couple of days. For the benefit of the complete novice, therefore, it is hoped that this chapter, which deals with the 'mechanics' of exhibiting, will clarify the situation and set uneasy minds at rest.

SHOW SCHEDULE

The first step, when contemplating showing birds, is to obtain a schedule for the appropriate show, and it is advisable initially to select one which is being held locally or within comfortable travelling distance. Practically all open shows in this country are advertised in the weekly journal *Cage and Aviary Birds* and the show schedule is obtained by writing (or telephoning) to the secretary of the cage bird society which is organising the show. A stamped, self-addressed envelope (large), or at least the postage stamp, will generally be appreciated for the reply as the total cost of staging a show these days is quite a burden on the usually slender resources of most societies. It is probably true to say that the majority of open bird shows in this country are run at a financial loss each year, and their continued existence is only ensured by the generous donations of fanciers and extra-curricular activities, such as tombola stalls and jumble sales.

As most shows stipulate a closing date for entries, which is usually about a week before the date of the show, in order to allow the organising committee to complete all the necessary paperwork and preparations, it is advisable to obtain your schedule as early as possible.

The show schedule for the typical open show will contain details of the classification, patronages (of which more will be said later), and prize lists for the various sections, which are normally Budgerigars, Canaries, British Birds, Foreign Birds, Bengalese and Zebra Finches. There are, of course, open shows which cater exclusively for Budgerigars or Canaries or one of the other sections but I shall assume that our budding exhibitor has avoided obtaining a schedule for one of these specialised shows, unless it is one for Foreign Birds only.

Patronage

It seems appropriate to consider the subject of patronage at this point, before proceeding further. At most open shows there are two forms of patronage — that granted by local cage bird societies and that granted by national or regional specialist societies.

Basically, the granting of patronage means that a society (local or national) has allocated a certain number of awards to be competed for at a particular show only by members of the society granting the patronage. The awards may take the form of rosettes, diplomas, trophies or, more rarely, cash. In the case of some of the national specialist societies, points are also allocated to any of their members exhibiting at patronage shows, and the exhibitors with the highest totals of points at the end of the show season usually receive one or more of the specialist societies' trophies.

The underlying reason for a show-promoting society seeking patronage is, of course, to increase the entry at their show by attracting members of the various societies, which have granted patronage, to exhibit. Whether or not this theory is actually sound in practice, in the case of local club patronage, is a debatable point. The majority of keen exhibitors, it appears, will show their birds at shows within their local area regardless of whether their own particular club has granted patronage or not. The prospect of winning an additional rosette in very limited competition is not likely to influence very many exhibitors, and the amount of work which devolves on organisers, stewards and judges as a result of having to select local patronage winners is, in my view, out of all proportion to the benefits (if any) to the exhibitors. However, if one is a member of a local cage bird society, which has granted its patronage to a particular show, one may as well indicate the fact on the entry form.

Novice exhibitors will also benefit from membership of one or more of the national specialist societies, including the **Foreign Bird Association, Foreign Bird League, Parrot Society, Australian Finch Society, Scottish Foreign Bird Society**, and others of a more regional basis. Apart from deriving a great deal of knowledge from these societies' publications, the exhibitor achieves personal contact with like-minded enthusiasts. Furthermore, some of the specialist societies mentioned above organise their own Club Shows which cater for the foreign bird exhibitor exclusively, and where the standard of competition is generally very high indeed.

Patronage granted to open shows by the national specialist societies is generally spread over events in many parts of the country in order that their widespread membership may have a fairly equitable opportunity of entering their birds.

Full details of all the societies, both local and national, which have granted patronage, will appear in the show schedule, including the names and addresses of their secretaries for the benefit of those non-members who may wish to join. Details of the awards, which they have allocated, are also included. Exhibitors, who intend nominating for patronage awards, are advised to read carefully through the schedule as the layout may vary for different societies. In some cases, all the foreign birds patronage awards are detailed at the commencement of the Foreign Bird Section, but, in others, all patronages are lumped together at the beginning or end of the schedule, particularly in the case of local patronages which generally cover more than one section. In order to simplify entries, the organising society will usually allocate a code number or group of initial letters to each patronage and, it is these initials or code numbers which must be entered in the appropriate column of the entry form, headed '*Nominations*'. The exhibitor must not, of course, nominate his entries for patronage awards if he is not a fully paid-up member of the relevant society. Returns showing the names of all patronage award winners must be made to each society at the conclusion of the show, by the show secretary.

Classification

To return to the show schedule, a study of the classification in the Foreign Bird Section will generally reveal a layout similar, but not necessarily identical, to that described in Chapter 1. The novice may be a little puzzled to note that, in every section of the schedule, with the exception of that for foreign birds, the classification is sub-divided into separate classes for **Champion** and **Novice** exhibitors (or more in the case of the Budgerigar section).

The reason for this is that the Foreign Bird Section is the only one in which the birds shown are predominantly wild-caught, whereas in all the other classes the birds have been bred in confinement. Furthermore, these varieties are being produced in an effort to attain a specific and detailed *show standard* and a great deal of skill and knowledge must be exercised by the breeder in his attempt to produce the ideal exhibit. This breeding expertise can only be acquired with experience and it would obviously be unfair to expect the novice exhibitor to be able to produce stock of the consistently high quality which the experienced champion might attain.

In the **Foreign Bird Section**, of course, the beginner can commence exhibiting in the Common Seedeater classes for example and progress to rarer and more delicate species as his experience grows. There is, therefore, less need for exhibitors to be divided into champion and novice categories as in the case of the domesticated species. The provision of champion and novice classes can, however, be seen in a very small number of show schedules in the foreign bird section, but as there is no formally recognised definition of champion and novice status in the foreign bird fancy, this is a rather pointless deviation from the norm.

Completing the Entry Form

Having carefully studied the classification in his schedule, the potential exhibitor then decides which of his stock he is going to enter, provided, of course, that he has ascertained that they are in perfect show condition. He then enters the numbers of the classes, in which he is entering, on the entry form (which he will have received with the schedule), together with the names of the species and details of his patronage nominations. Most entry forms also have a column in which the exhibitor may, if he so wishes, enter the prices at which he wishes to sell his exhibits, excluding the show cage. Relatively few foreign bird exhibitors, however, wish to sell the birds they have entered and generally write 'Not for Sale' in this column. Where birds are sold under such circumstances a commis-

CERTIFICATE OF ENTRY

Number of Class	This Col for Sec. use only	Checked In and Out	DESCRIPTION OF ENTRY *Kindly use one line for each Entry.*	Nomination Column	Selling Price Excluding Packing £	p.

In making the above Entries I declare the above Specimens are *bona fide* my own property and I agree to abide by the Rules and Regulations of the above Show, also any birds shown by me will be shown in conformity with the Birds Protection Act, 1954. I also certify that the birds exhibited by me in the Budgerigar Breeders Classes were bred by me and are wearing my own Official Closed Coded Ring for the current year purchased from the Budgerigar Society through the General Secretary. I enclose £ , the amount required to enable me to exhibit.

Signed...

Please write clearly and distinctly, and state whether Mr., Mrs. or Miss.

		£	p.
Entry Fees	..................at		
	..................at		
	..................at		
	..................at		
Catalogue	..................at		
	£		

NAME (in Block Letters)...

FULL ADDRESS...

....

Entries to :— The Secretary,

No. Rail Tickets......................

All Postal Orders etc. to be made payable to :—

Date 19

Nominated Society ....

8.1 **Certificate of Entry**

sion fee — usually 10 per cent of the selling price — will be charged by the society.

Finally, the exhibitor must sign the entry form, after inserting his name and address — it is not unknown for these latter details to be omitted! The entry form must then be returned to the show secretary together with the appropriate remittance to cover the total entry fee. Within a few days, the exhibitor will receive his cage labels; these are the small gummed labels which are inscribed with the number of the class and the number which has been allocated to the fancier's entry in that class. At the same time he will also be supplied with a 'packing card' listing the numbers of all his entries, which must be affixed inside his carrying case, and address labels if the entries are to be sent or returned by rail.

While the beginner should make every effort to ensure that his entry form has been completed accurately, there may be occasions when he will enter one of his exhibits in the wrong class. In other sections of the show — Budgerigar, Canary for example — the judge will 'wrong class' an incorrect entry, which means, in effect, that the exhibit is excluded from the competition and the entry fee forfeited. However, the majority of show schedules state that no entries in the Foreign Section will be 'wrong classed', so that the novice exhibitor need not worry even if he does slip up. If a foreign species is found to be entered in the wrong class, it will generally be transferred to the correct class and the cage label suitably altered.

Junior Exhibitors

Although all adult exhibitors must show their exotic species in the same classes, there are separate classes provided for Junior exhibitors at virtually every show. The number and variety of classes laid on for Juniors may vary from a single '**Any Variety Foreign**' to as many as five, or more, providing separate cover for Common and Rare Seedeaters, Parrot-like, Softbills and Current-year Bred.

There is no official requirement, of course, that a Junior must exhibit in Junior classes, unless this is specifically stipulated in the show rules of any individual show-promoting society. Although it seems advisable for Juniors to work their way up the ladder by gaining experience in the classes allocated to them, they may compete in the adult classes if they so wish. There is a real risk, however, that disappointment may lead the unsuccessful ones to retire,

8.2 **Gouldian Finches** (*Chloebia gouldiae*) Length $5\frac{1}{2}$ inches (14 cm)
Considered by many as the most desirable of all the Australian seedeaters. Named by the renowned naturalist John Gould in honour of his wife Elizabeth. The wings and mantle are grass-green, rump and upper tail-coverts bright blue. A large area of lilac adorns the upper breast contrasting vividly with the rich yellow lower breast and abdomen, and the black throat patch. The crown of the head and cheeks are scarlet, although there are two varieties, both occuring in the wild, in which the scarlet head colouring is replaced by black or orange-yellow. The taxonomic position of the Gouldian Finch is not wholly agreed: considered by some to represent a link between the Parrot-finches and the Munias. Because Gouldian Finches are being bred in such considerable numbers it is essential to select only top quality specimens for the show team.

disillusioned, from exhibiting at an early age.

As foreign bird exhibiting is not governed by any one nationally-recognised body, there is no official definition of Junior status. It is generally accepted, however, that a Junior is an exhibitor who has not attained his sixteenth birthday. Where a Junior reaches the age of sixteen during a show season it is usually recognised that he may continue to exhibit as a Junior until the end of that show season.

Quite a large number of show-promoting societies also stipulate in their show rules that exhibitors in the Junior section are not eligible to compete for adult awards. In other words, a Junior's exhibit may take the award for **Best Junior Foreign** Bird or **Best Junior Exhibit**, but it will not be allowed to compete for the **Best Foreign Exhibit** or **Best Bird in Show**.

It is quite inexplicable why some societies discriminate against Junior exhibitors in this way. It is true that the entry fee in the Junior section is generally less than that in the open classes, but this fact is usually reflected in the smaller amount of class prize money which is allocated to the Juniors. Awards for, say, **Best Parrot-like, Best Foreign Bird in Show** and so on are surely only really valid and worthwhile if all exhibits in the relevant categories— including those entered by Juniors — are taken into consideration when the winners are being selected. If an exhibit is good enough to receive an award, in the opinion of the judge, it is surely of no consequence whether the exhibitor is older than sixteen years or younger. It is pleasing that there are a number of show-promoting societies which share this point of view.

While on the subject of Junior exhibitors, perhaps the complaint, which is heard fairly frequently at open shows, should be mentioned, of Juniors 'borrowing' one of their parent's better birds to enter in the Junior classes, in order to increase their chances of winning.

It is apparent that such occurrences do take place and I have personally witnessed a particular bird being entered in a Junior class at one show, and then being exhibited a few weeks later at another show by the previous exhibitor's father. As a parent myself, I can understand the desire of other parents who wish to see their offspring doing well in the same pastime, but their efforts are misdirected if they try and achieve success in this way.

It is also grossly unfair on the many genuine Junior exhibitors,

8.3 **Festive Tanager** (*Tangara cyanocephala*) Length 5½ inches (14 cm)
A rare Softbill from South America, also known as the Red-necked Tanager. Less frequently imported than some of the others of the *Tangara* genus which numbers some 47 species. This genus provides some of the most beautifully-coloured Tanagers to be seen on the show bench.

whose parents are not in the least interested in aviculture, and who have to finance and care for their hard-won exhibits with the aid of their limited pocket money. It is very disappointing to witness youngsters turning up at open shows with some of the commoner species, such as Silverbills and Cut-throats, which they have enthusiastically cared for in person, only to find that they may be competing against some rare Softbill, 'borrowed' from an over-indulgent parent.

There are many bird fanciers who deliberately encourage their sons and daughters to take up a variety different to that kept by the parents. In this way, there is no temptation for the youngsters to show birds other than their own. However, it would also be quite understandable that a youngster would want to keep and exhibit the same species as his parent, particularly in the case of foreign birds, where there is such a wide field of choice. In such cases, it is to be hoped that parents would encourage the young fancier to look after and exhibit only his own birds.

THE SHOW

The next step in the procedure followed by the budding enthusiast in getting his birds onto the show bench, having obtained the cage labels, is to ascertain from the schedule the deadline by which his exhibits must be handed in at the show venue. It is assumed for the moment that the novice has selected, for his first show, one which is within easy reach and to which he can personally convey his exhibits.

Benching the bird

Most show schedules stipulate that all birds must be benched by nine o'clock on the morning of the show, or occasionally before this where judging is to commence earlier than usual. At the same time, it is usually stated that the show venue will be manned during the evening — and sometimes the afternoon — on the day before the show, for the benefit of fanciers who wish to bring their exhibits along at those times.

It seems preferable to convey birds to a show on the previous evening as this allows plenty of time to prepare the cages, and also enables the birds at least some time to become accustomed to the noise and bustle of the show venue, rather than being thrust in front of the judge within a fairly short time of being caught up from the flight or stock cage. A mad scramble to catch birds for an early morning dash to a show venue can also lead to damage to the birds' plumage, which could ruin their chances on the show bench for the rest of the season.

The exhibitor need have no qualms about leaving his birds overnight at the show venue. They will be well cared for and the majority of societies employ night stewards who generally sleep in the show hall in order to protect the exhibits from prowlers of whatever ilk. This brings to mind an amusing incident which was described by a member of a **West Country Cage Bird Society**, which stages one of the largest shows in the South West of England. On the evening before the show, when all the exhibits had seen safely installed on the staging, the night stewards were getting ready to dim the lights before settling down for the night, when they heard the mewing of a cat from somewhere within the hall. Several diligent, if rather frantic, searches failed to reveal any sign of a feline intruder although the mewing was still heard intermittently. The stewards were almost at the point of distraction when they finally discovered that the culprit was, in fact, one of the exhibits — a talented Indian Hill Mynah which had been imitating the miaow of a cat to perfection! The comments of the stewards are not on record!

Labelling

Before conveying the birds to the show venue, it is essential to ensure that the cage labels are firmly fixed to the front bottom rails of the show cages. The backs of the cage labels are gummed and, while it is usually only necessary to moisten them, there are occasions when they become detached from the show cage. To avoid this it is advisable to affix the labels with a reliable adhesive rather than rely on the moistened gum. I would not recommend that transparent adhesive tape be used for this purpose as this will render it difficult for the judge to write on the cage labels, and could also result in the exhibit being regarded as a 'marked' cage.

Some cage bird societies use show cage labels for their foreign bird entries, which have a blank space at the bottom marked **'species'**, the idea being that the name of the species is displayed for the benefit of the general public and less experienced fanciers. The responsibility for entering the name of the species in this space varies from show to show. In some cases the show secretary will do so before sending out the cage labels, using the information as to the species which should be included on the entry form. In other instances the show secretary may rely on the exhibitor to enter the name of the species before affixing the cage labels to his cages. Although obviously an exhibitor may, for various reasons, change his mind as to which species he is going to enter in a particular class, between the time he sends off his entry form and the date of the show, on balance it seems that this responsibility should rest with the show secretary using the information supplied to him on the exhibitors' entry forms. It is wise to add that there is no official requirement for either party to insert the name of the species on such cage labels, nor even that this type of cage label be used in the Foreign Bird Section. It is simply a courtesy gesture which must add to the general public's enjoyment of the show.

Transporting the Exhibits

In the case of shows being held fairly locally, the majority of exhibitors will convey their birds to the venue in the luggage compartment or rear seat of their cars. It is advisable that the show cages should be placed in a secure container, which will prevent overturning, disturbance to the birds from headlights and street lighting (if transported in the evening) and sudden cold draughts and extreme variations in temperature.

Some fanciers utilise suitable cardboard boxes for containing their show cages but, while these may be satisfactory as a temporary measure for local shows, it is advisable to obtain properly constructed wooden carrying cases, into which the show cages will fit snugly. Details of carrying case construction will be found in Chapter 6.

If show cages are to be sent to the show venue other than by private car, then it is essential that proper carrying cases are used. The novice exhibitor, having obtained some experience at local shows, will, sooner or later, decide to exhibit at some of the larger shows which may be held at a venue many miles from his home. In such cases it is usually impracticable for the fancier to transport his exhibits to the show venue personally and rail or commercial road transport must, therefore, be arranged.

A number of years ago it was a fairly simple matter to send birds to a show by rail and the facility was widely available. Today, the closure of many small railway stations, together with the more stringent regulations governing the conveyance of livestock, has restricted this service to the fancier to a point where it is virtually non-existent in many cases. Where the nearest, manned railway station is a considerable number of miles from the show venue, as is often the case nowadays, many societies find it impossible to accept entries which would have to be sent by rail. It is therefore essential that the exhibitor, who intends sending his birds in this way, should study the show schedule carefully to ensure that the organising society is in a position to accept rail birds.

British Rail will not accept livestock for conveyance in situations where the consignment is likely to arrive at its destination after 4 p.m. on Fridays unless special arrangements have been made to collect the livestock at the receiving station. This restriction is designed to prevent the possibility of livestock being deprived of proper attention during the weekend if not collected promptly by the consignee. As the vast majority of bird shows are held on Saturdays and/or Sundays, of course, the society organising the show must ensure that their local station will receive the birds and that each train is met so that the birds may be immediately taken to the show venue.

The exhibitor must indicate on his entry form, in appropriate cases, that he proposes sending his birds by rail and also that they are to be returned by rail, or otherwise as the case may be. In some instances the exhibitor may send his birds by rail and then visit the show on the last day, thereby enabling him to bring back his exhibits by car. In such cases only one set of rail labels will be required for the outward journey. These rail labels are supplied by the show-promoting society and are forwarded to the fancier along with his cage labels, after receipt of his entry form. The labels are specially designed for the purpose and incorporate a removable flap, or top cover, which is tucked into a slot in the main portion of the label.

The name of the consignee and the railway station from which the birds are to be collected are written on the top flap (usually by the show secretary), while the name of the sender and the return destination must be inserted on the part of the label underneath the flap, by the exhibitor. It is then a simple matter for the show stewards to tear off the top flap when preparing the exhibits for their return journey at the end of the show.

In cases where birds are being sent to a show and also returned from there by rail, the sender, that is the exhibitor, must pay for both journeys at the time of initial despatch.

There are many fanciers, of course, who do not have access to rail transport facilities, and others who do may find the costs prohibitive if they intend entering a reasonable number of birds. Quite a considerable number of cage bird societies now organise transport for their members' exhibits — particularly in the case of the larger shows such as the **National** — by hiring a large van and

8.4 **Diamond Firetails** (*Zonaeginthus guttatus*) Length $4\frac{3}{4}$ inches (12 cm)
Excellent species for the show team — hardy and easy to cater for. The members of the *Zonaeginthus* genus are regarded aviculturally as difficult, but the Diamond Firetail (also referred to as the Diamond Sparrow, which it is not) is the exception to the rule. Not too difficult to breed and one of the most popular of Australian seedeaters. It is however inclined to become over-fat if housed in restricted accommodation and should be provided with a roomy aviary.

A J Simpson,
Canary & Cage Bird Life

collecting the birds at various 'picking-up points' in the locality. As the van is usually manned by members of the society, this system has the advantage that the birds are in the care of experienced fanciers for the whole of the time, and the cost of conveyance per cage is usually much less than in the case of carriage by rail. Even if the exhibitor's own local cage bird society does not arrange transport of this nature, it is sometimes possible to take up any surplus space which may be available in a vehicle belonging to a neighbouring society and local enquiries may prove fruitful.

Judging

Having safely delivered his exhibits to the show venue by one means or another, the exhibitor will naturally be anxious to find out, as soon as possible, how successful they have proved. While judging is taking place, only officials, judges and stewards are allowed inside the hall and the general public (including exhibitors) are excluded until the judges have completed their task. Although many novices would no doubt wish to watch their birds being assessed this would be completely impracticable at most venues, bearing in mind the fact that several hundreds of birds have to be carried to and from the judging stands, and also that a considerable amount of paperwork passes between the judges, stewards and secretary's table during the actual judging procedure. If a few hundred eager exhibitors were to be added to such a situation, the task of judges and officials would be quite hopeless.

At most shows, the judging will have been completed by lunchtime on the first day, or very soon thereafter, and the general public are usually admitted at about two or three o'clock. When I have been judging at a show, I always make a point of remaining in the hall for two or three hours after it has been opened to the public, so that exhibitors — particularly the beginners — can approach me, if they so wish, to find out why I have placed the birds in a particular order.

There will be many occasions when the novice exhibitor will be disappointed with the results he achieves, and even the experienced fancier will disagree with the judge's decisions from time to time. Any judge, who is worthy of the name, will be only too pleased to discuss his opinions and reasons for his choice of winners, if asked in a polite and non-aggressive manner. Judges are not infallible, but a bad loser in any form of competition is never popular, and the judge's decisions should be accepted as having been reached with honesty and impartiality.

The novice should also take the opportunity, at every show he attends, to study carefully all the exhibits in the foreign section and to try and observe the reasons why some have been highly placed and others not. It is only in this way that a good, all-round knowledge of other species and the general exhibition standard of all the birds can be acquired. It is as well to remember that one's own exhibits have been judged *in relation to* the other birds in their class or section and not in isolation.

Collecting Procedure

At the end of the show the exhibitor, if present in person, will no doubt be impatient to collect his birds (and trophies, if any) and he will usually find that the time when exhibits may be lifted, that is removed from the staging, is stipulated in the show schedule. It is necessary to follow the collecting procedure laid down by the organisers, not because there is very much risk of birds being removed dishonestly, but to prevent the accidental removal of the wrong exhibits, which can readily occur in the general bustle and confusion, where the same species are involved.

Most societies utilise the exhibitor's lifting card or entry form as the basis of their lifting procedure. The lifting card is simply a list of the exhibitor's entries, described by class and cage numbers only, which is sent to him along with his cage labels. Where exhibits are being returned to the owner by rail, or being collected by a third party, the lifting card should be securely fixed inside the lid of the carrying case which contains the show cages, before despatch to the show.

There appears to be a growing trend, however, for show organisers to use the exhibitor's entry form as a security check during the removal of birds at the end of show. In these cases the exhibitor must collect his entry form from the show secretary before removing his show cages from the staging, and, at the same time, receive any prize money which may be due to him, if it has not already been distributed during the day.

Having retrieved his entry form, the fancier must then gather together all his exhibits and take them to one of the check-out points which may be designated by the exhibitors' initials or the variety of bird being exhibited. It is advisable, before placing the show cages into their carrying case, to empty the water from the drinking receptacles into one of the buckets, or other facility provided by the organisers, to prevent spillage in transit.

The entry form must be handed to the steward at the check-out table and the show cages removed from their carrying cases so that he may confirm that the numbers on the cage labels correspond with those on the form. When the steward has signed the entry form, the exhibitor is then free to remove his exhibits from the hall.

Prizes

The novice exhibitor, who achieves some success on the show bench for the first time, may be somewhat surprised at the meagre amount of prize money which he receives. Prizes at competitive bird shows are divided into two categories:

1. **Class prize money**
2. **Specials.**

Class prize money, which is generally calculated on a sliding scale, is based on a percentage of the amounts received in entry fees in each class. This will, of course, vary according to the number of entries per class, and prize money is usually paid to the exhibits which are placed first, second and third in the class — or first and second only where there are less than four entries. Classes which contain only a single entry generally receive a prize card but no cash award. Almost invariably, class prize money will comprise of pence rather than pounds.

The term '**Specials**' is applied to all awards other than class prizes, and includes cash, rosettes, plaques, etc. which may be allocated for **Best in Show, Best in Section, Best Parrot-like** and similar categories. Although a number of handsome prizes are included in the specials list of some of the larger shows each season, the cash value of the award for **Best Foreign Bird in Show** will normally be in the range of five to ten pounds, with additional prizes of around one to two pounds for **Best Seedeater** and so on. In order to acquire this sort of cash award, an exhibit will certainly have to beat scores, or even hundreds, of competitors.

Bearing in mind the costs involved in transporting birds to a show venue, it will be very apparent to readers that exhibitors of

---

8.5 Mr. and Mrs G. Sharratt, of Chellaston, receive the **Supreme Trophy at the 1980 National Exhibition of Cage and Aviary Birds**. This most-coveted of awards was won by their immaculate Royal Starling.

foreign birds do not indulge in this pastime with a view to monetary gain.

So far, this chapter has described the typical, if rather formal, procedures which the exhibitor will generally be required to follow at open shows. Many cage bird societies, however, also stage Members' Shows and Table Shows and these are most useful, giving the beginner an insight into showing and show organisation. These are usually informal affairs, where entries are restricted to members of the society only, and with exhibitors often being expected to participate in the organisation of the event.

Any prizes allocated at these small shows are usually of nominal value but a good deal of knowledge and enjoyment may be derived from participation. In most instances, of course, the classification will be very much more limited than that provided at open shows and may be restricted to only four Foreign Bird classes, e.g.:

1. **Any Variety Common Seedeater**
2. **Any Variety Rare Seedeater**
3. **Any Variety Parrot-like**
4. **Any Variety of Softbill.**

THE NATIONAL

This chapter on exhibiting cannot be concluded without making some reference to the most popular show in this country — the **National Exhibition of Cage and Aviary Birds**. It may be argued that a few specialist shows provide a greater degree of competition in certain individual sections, but in terms of the open, all-varieties show the National, as it is popularly called, is without doubt the biggest and the best.

Attracting over seven thousand exhibits of many different varieties, the National is the *Mecca* for bird fanciers from all over the world, who come to see the cream of this country's show stock. As the leading exhibition, the National does not seek the patronage of any of the specialist societies, but all the important societies are invited to submit nominations for the appointment of judges for the various sections, and these nominations are considered by the organising committee when making their selection.

No class prize money is awarded at the National and the cash prizes in the specials' list are, on the whole, of limited value; but certificates are awarded to the winners of the first to seventh places

8.6 A coveted **First Prize Certificate awarded at 'The National'**, the highlight of the show season for most exhibitors, and with an entry of 7–8000 exhibits from all over the British Isles, competition is of a high standard.

in each class and the prestige and glory of winning a National certificate is ample reward.

In addition to being the largest exhibition of cage and aviary birds in the country, the National is also the longest, and generally extends over the period comprising Friday, Saturday and Sunday. In order to allow for possible minor delays most exhibitors will despatch their birds to the National by road or rail on the Thursday morning and they may not be returned until some time on the Monday. This is a rather long and exhausting experience for any bird, and only those of perfect physical fitness should be subjected to it.

Apart from the competitive aspect of the National, a number of specialist societies also take the opportunity to hold their Annual General Meetings while the show is taking place, which gives fanciers the opportunity of meeting fellow enthusiasts from many different parts of the country. There are also a large number of trade stands on view, allowing the foreign bird fancier the facility

of examining and purchasing a wide range of exotic species, both rare and common.

8.7 **A general view of part of the 1980 National**. The venue for this event was switched to Bingley Hall, Birmingham after the disastrous fire which destroyed Alexandra Palace in 1980.

CHAPTER 9

Shows and Standards

ROLE OF SHOWS

Many thousands of foreign bird enthusiasts derive enormous pleasure from keeping and breeding exotic species, without ever participating in exhibitions. Indeed, if one examines the total membership figures of the national specialist societies catering for the various exotic species, and compares those with the number of members who actually exhibit at patronage shows, it will be found that the exhibitors form a fairly small percentage of the total. The actual percentage varies from society to society, but figures of 5 per cent or less are not unusual.

We must, therefore, accept that exhibiting is a minority pursuit, but, at the same time, we must recognise that its devotees are dedicated and enthusiastic, and derive a considerable amount of pleasure and benefit from their participation. As both an exhibitor and a judge I have certainly enjoyed immensely the friendliness and good-natured rivalry at many shows.

Benefits

What, then, is to be gained by showing birds? In some spheres of bird-keeping, where the breeding and selling of quality exhibition stock has virtually become a business enterprise, it is essential for the breeder to exhibit **and win** regularly in order to demonstrate and maintain the market value of his stock. Happily, such a state of affairs does not appertain in the Foreign Bird Fancy where a bird's worth is judged by its scarcity or breeding potential, rather than its ability to win rosettes. I believe that the majority of exhibitors in the Foreign section participate mainly from a simple desire to compete — in the same way and for the same reason that others choose to indulge on a competitive basis in football, cricket, angling or other sport. It is the will to win, a fancier's desire to prove that his or her stock is as good as, or superior to, that possessed by other fanciers, which draws the exhibitor to the shows each season. It is certainly not the prospect of financial reward which attracts, for exhibiting exotic species can truly be said to be an amateur pursuit.

One of the fringe benefits of exhibiting, or which some may regard as the major benefit, is the opportunity of meeting fellow enthusiasts. If exhibitors study the entries and compare notes on their breeding successes and failures a great deal of valuable information can be disseminated at show venues. The fancier who is only interested in collecting rosettes and trophies at any price will derive very little real benefit from showing his stock and will not endear himself to fellow exhibitors.

STANDARDS

It must always be remembered that small livestock exhibiting is a hobby and as such must be undertaken for fun and pleasure. Where show *standards* are stipulated by specialist societies, let us remember that these are arbitrary criteria set down by a committee of fallible humans. These *standards* are subject to change from time to time and, more importantly, they are also subject to the individual interpretation of the judge. In the case of the exhibiting of exotic **species** we do not even have the flimsy guidelines of official show *standards* to aid the adjudicator in his difficult task. How then can we do other than acknowledge that the judges' decisions have been made in good faith and accept them in a mature and sporting manner.

The lack of descriptive show *standards* for exotic species is a subject which frequently evokes discussion and sometimes puzzles the novice exhibitor. Although all other sections of the Fancy have their specific show *standards*, only the domesticated Bengalese and Zebra Finch are similarly catered for in the exotic sphere. It is, in fact, rather misleading to regard the Bengalese as a foreign species as it has been domesticated for very much longer than the Budgerigar. Bengalese were domesticated some two centuries ago by the Japanese, whereas the Budgerigar was first imported into Britain as a wild-caught Grass Parrakeet as recently as 1840 by the accomplished naturalist John Gould.

Criteria for Exotic Species

However, when considering the volume and diversity of exotic species which have been imported into Europe in recent years, it would obviously be an impossible task to attempt to formulate a detailed show standard for each individual species. Furthermore, there is no single specialist society which has been in a position to act as governing body in the foreign bird sphere. At the present time, in addition to national societies such as the **Foreign Bird Association, Foreign Bird League, Australian Finch Society** and **Parrot Society**, there is an ever increasing number of regionally based societies which, may, however, draw their membership from all parts of the country. Such societies include the **Scottish Foreign Bird Society**, the **Welsh Foreign, Zebra Finch** and **Bengalese Society,** the **Midland Foreign Bird Association,** the **Southern Foreign Bird Club** and so on.

If any attempt were to be made to establish show *standards* for exotic species, it seem likely that the majority (or perhaps, all) of the specialist societies would wish to participate in the deliberations. In fact, it would be essential that they did so, in order to formulate a nationally recognised set of *standards*. Any attempt by splinter groups or dissentients to establish their own standards would create an impossible situation for judges and exhibitors alike.

As noted earlier it would be quite impracticable to try and draw up a show *standard* for each individual species covering such details as type, colour, markings, and other requirements. However, it may not be very difficult to formulate a *general standard* for the guidance of exhibitors and judges, which could be applicable to all species. At the present time there are no official guidelines for the judges of foreign species, except that certain criteria have become established by tradition and common usage.

ASSESSING SPECIES

It is generally accepted that, when judging foreign species, the judge must take into account the basic factors of **condition, quality** and **rarity**. Unfortunately, the order of precedence may vary according to the inclinations of the individual judge with resultant confusion among fanciers. It would, therefore, be most useful if the specialist societies were to get together to establish a standard or code which, perhaps by means of points allocation, would indicate

9.1 **Three-coloured Tanager** (*Tangara tricolour*)
A beautiful Brazilian Softbill needing great care to reach perfect show condition. Requires a varied fruit diet supplemented by an insectile mixture and livefood.

those features to which emphasis would have to be given when giving awards.

However, that is a hope for the future; for the present the judge must use his discretion and experience in selecting the winners. In my own case, when adjudicating in the foreign section, I first give consideration to **condition**, and I am sure that many other judges do likewise.

Condition

The condition of the bird is viewed, in fact, in two separate ways:

1. **physiological fitness**
2. **physical perfection, free of flaw or defect.**

As far as fitness is concerned, no exhibit should be considered for an award unless it is obviously healthy. On the other hand, birds which possess some defect such as damaged plumage or missing claws must be judged against the merits of the other entries in the class.

Quality

Having assessed the condition of the entries, the judge must then consider their **quality**. In the case of non-standardised species, which are virtually all those in the foreign section, quality depends on whether or not the exhibit is a good representative example of its own species. In the case of pairs, matching of the two birds by size and shade of colour will also have to be taken into account. Quality is *not* synonymous with size although, alas, some judges appear to take this attitude.

In almost every section of bird exhibiting today, bigger has been regarded as being better. Whether or not the bulky Budgerigars and Canaries currently seen on the show bench are aesthetically superior to their more petite antecedents is for their respective devotees to judge. In my view, the diminutive size of many of the species is one of their most attractive qualities, and it therefore appears to be quite illogical to endeavour to increase that size beyond natural limits. Furthermore, most fanciers will be aware that, in the case of those exotic birds which are distributed over a wide range, there may occur several geographical races of the same species.

These races may, generally, be differentiated by slight variations in size and/or colour, and some of the African species provide good examples of this. In a number of commonly imported species, such as the Red-billed Firefinch (*Lagonosticta senegala*), the Cordon Bleu (*Uraeginthus bengalus*), Green Singing Finch (*Serinus mozambicus*) and others, the East or South African races are somewhat larger than those from more western areas. Consequently, almost the entire West African populations of some species are handicapped, if we regard size as an important criterion of perfection. This seems a perfectly ludicrous situation, and judges must recognise and make allowance for the fact that there is a considerable variation in size among geographical races and sub-species in certain cases.

The absurdity of this obsession with size was well illustrated for me by an occurrence at a local show some years ago, where I was both exhibiting and assisting in the organisation. When the judging had been completed, the foreign section judge approached me to explain why the awards in one of the classes had been altered on his judging slip. He informed me that he had allocated the class prizes when it was discovered that one of the exhibits in that particular class was missing. The mislaid bird was found and brought forward

9.2 **Roseate Cockatoo** (*Cacatua roseicapilla*)
This beautiful pink-and-grey Australian species is known in its homeland as the Galah. In Australia it is regarded as a menace to crops and may be killed by farmers, while the ban on its export ensures that it remains a rarity in European aviculture.

for judging, whereupon it was awarded first prize because, explained the judge, it was much bigger than the specimen he had previously placed first. Consternation at the judge's explanation is quite understandable when it is pointed out that the bird, which was originally allocated first place, was a male Half-Masked Weaver (*Ploceus velatus vitellinus*) whereas the missing exhibit, which eventually took the honours, was a male Ruppell's Golden Weaver.

Admittedly there is a similarity in colour and pattern of plumage in the case of these two species, but the disparity in size is such that even the most inexperienced of judges should have realised that these were two quite separate species, and the question of comparative size just did not enter into the competition.

Rarity

The third factor which is generally considered to be one of the basic criteria in judging foreign birds is **rarity**. Many judges appear to place considerable emphasis on this particular aspect when

9.3 **Leadbeater's Cockatoo** (*Cacatua leadbeateri*)
An Australian species, only rarely available to aviculturists in this country. It possesses the most magnificent tricoloured crest. All cockatoos are very noisy and tend to be difficult subjects to stage in perfect feather.

selecting their winners, but the logic of this approach has always eluded me. It must be remembered that when the rarity of a particular species is referred to in this context, it does not mean that it is an endangered species which is scarce in the wild, but only that it is rarely available to aviculture in this country. The reasons for the scarcity may be several and varied — political or military unrest, government conservation policies, transport problems, access difficulties and so on.

In Australia, for example, the Galah, better known to fanciers in this country as the Roseate Cockatoo, is so numerous in some areas that it is allowed to be slaughtered as an agricultural pest, while the Australian government's blanket ban on fauna exports results in the same bird being regarded as an avicultural rarity outside its own country. Because some of the factors which influence a species' availability are variable, the scarcity or otherwise of that species may be sporadic. Occasionally a species which has been 'lost' to aviculture for years will suddenly appear on the market and be freely available, although perhaps only for a relatively short time.

Whatever the reason for any species being classified as '*rare*' it is hard to see how this can be used as a criterion for assessing the superiority of the bird on the show bench. When judging, what is being looked for is physical perfection in relation to the individual species being examined, and the fact that a particular species may or may not be readily available to fanciers can have no bearing on its intrinsic quality. Rarity can only enhance the monetary value of a bird, and even then the effect is understandable rather than excusable.

FURTHER CRITERIA IN ASSESSING SPECIES

At any bird show, of course, where there is a reasonable number of entries in the foreign section, a few may be of outstanding condition and quality, while others will, very obviously, fall far below these high standards. The majority of the exhibits, however, will generally be found to be of approximately equal merit in terms of condition and quality, and further criteria must, therefore, be applied in order to indicate the winning entries.

Show Condition

One factor which should be considered in this respect is the difficulty, or otherwise, of achieving and maintaining show condition in a particular species. Other judges, no doubt, also take this into account, but it seems that in many cases judging whether a bird is difficult to maintain has been confused with its rarity. It is, of course, quite erroneous to assume that all rare birds are difficult to keep in confinement. As noted earlier, the reasons for the scarcity of any species in aviculture may be diverse, but a delicate constitution is not, generally, a major cause. Frequently, when rare species become available, it is found that they are as easy to cater for as some of the commonly imported examples.

Although there is, therefore, no virtue in *rarity*, it is notably more difficult to groom some species into show condition than others. This difficulty may arise from a number of contributory factors, including feather texture, feather size, plumage pattern, and diet. Consequently, the fancier who has the harder task to attain show condition must be given due credit when his exhibits warrant a top award.

9.4 **Long-Tailed Grassfinches** (*Poephila acuticauda*)
One of the most popular of the Australian grassfinches; very attractive, although lacking gaudy colours. For exhibition specimens the two elongated central tail-feathers should be as long as possible and this point should also be borne in mine when selecting breeding pairs with a view to producing exhibition stock.

Larger species, such as Touracos, Pies and Parrots, tend to be more susceptible to plumage damage than the smaller birds and, in these larger birds, any feather defects are, of course, far more easily discernible by the judge. Similarly, those species which have proportionately long tails are more difficult to stage in *feather perfect* condition, and this must be recognised by the judge when assessing the relative merits of the exhibits. Consequently such species as Parrakeets, Whydahs and Colies, for example, should benefit slightly in relation to short-tailed species, if they are exhibited with perfect tails — all other aspects being equal, of course.

The knowledgeable judge should give due consideration to the relative difficulties involved in bringing all the various species into show condition. These difficulties are, it should again be stressed, in no way related to the rarity of the species in question.

Exhibitor–Bred Birds

One point of controversy which sometimes arises in judging circles is the practice of giving precedence to exhibits which have been *bred*. This attitude is frequently encountered when one is judging the best bird from each section for the coveted, but often controversial, award of **Best In Show**. On such occasions the Budgerigar and/or Canary judges will often nominate the best birds from their respective sections on the grounds that they have been bred by fanciers whereas the foreign section winner has not. This attitude is quite obviously ludicrous, for the following reasons:

1. **There is no way that a judge may reasonably ascertain that any bird bred in confinement was, in fact, so produced in the exhibitor's aviary (except of course in the case of exhibits emanating from *Breeder classes*, where only birds wearing coded, closed rings are eligible for entry).**
2. **No judge can state with certainty, that an exhibit in the foreign section has *not* been bred in confinement.**

Today more foreign birds are being bred by aviculturists than ever before, but, because of the risks involved, many such birds are not *close-rung* by their breeders and are, therefore, not eligible to compete in breeders' classes. Consequently, the open classes at many shows often contain a number of exhibits, bred by fanciers, which are indistinguishable from the imported birds. Furthermore, the upsurge of interest in Australian seedeaters has resulted in many examples of these species appearing on the show bench, and these are indisputably, and necessarily, bred in confinement as a result of the Australian ban on fauna export.

It can, of course, be argued that the fact that an exhibit has been bred by the exhibitor is worthy of recognition, and this does seem to be receiving the attention of show-promoting societies, inasmuch as there has been a considerable increase in the number of **Breeders' Classes** and **Specials** in the foreign sections of many shows in the past few years. However, the mere fact that a particular exhibit has been bred in confinement, whereas others may have been wild-caught, is totally irrelevant in relation to its merit on the show bench.

Steadiness in a Bird

Perhaps one of the most important attributes which any avian exhibit should possess is **steadiness**. All the other qualities of a bird can only be seen to advantage by the judge when it shows itself well.

It is not difficult to appreciate that, when transferred from an aviary into a relatively tiny show cage and then transported to a noisy, bustling show hall, the inexperienced bird will be subjected to considerable stress. The symptoms of such stress may vary according to the species. Lovebirds, for example, will attempt to dig a 'funk hole' for themselves in a corner of the cage with an Ostrich-like obsession to blot out reality, while the Weaver family, on the other hand, throw themselves around the cage and dash against the bars in wild panic. Firefinches tend to 'freeze' on the perch in a head-down posture, like that assumed by the European Wren, in contrast to the larger Parrots which growl belligerently at anyone who ventures too near their cages.

Different individuals of the same species may vary in their reaction to the stresses of the show bench, and, in any event, the average foreign exhibit should not be expected to be as rock-steady as, say, a well trained Yorkshire Canary. Apart, however, from the fact that untrained birds can fray and damage their plumage in their panic, it is essential that the judge is afforded a reasonable opportunity to study the exhibits in some detail, and this he cannot do if they are scrabbling on the floor or dashing around the cage. Ideally, therefore, the exhibit, regardless of species, should be alert, fearless and completely devoid of any excessive activity induced by stress.

CHAPTER 10

Judge for Yourself

Sooner or later the majority of Foreign Bird exhibitors will either experience a desire to 'try' judging, or, as they become recognised as experienced exhibitors, they will be asked to officiate at one of the local shows.

A JUDGE'S QUALIFICATIONS

In this country, judges of exotic species do not receive any formal training and are not examined by any official body. They are not required to belong to any particular specialist society and their recognition as competent judges is based solely on their personal reputations. If a judge carries out his engagements fairly and efficiently, in a manner which indicates that he has a sound knowledge of Foreign Bird exhibiting, his reputation will slowly spread until he is being invited to officiate at some of the major shows.

Whether this is a satisfactory system of acquiring competent judges is open to debate. It is undoubtedly true that there are fanciers officiating at shows who are hopelessly incompetent as judges of exotic species. At many smaller shows I have often seen the judging of the Foreign Bird section being carried out by the Budgerigar judge. In fact it is not unknown for some unenlightened Budgerigar judges, or show committee members, to express the view that judging the Foreign section is a simple task as there are no *official show standards* and the birds have to be judged purely on condition. At those shows where the best bird from each section is brought forward to compete for a **Best Bird in Show** award, it is often revealing and somewhat dismaying to hear the comments of the other Section judges when they are trying to assess the merits of the **Best Foreign Exhibit**. It should be hastily added, however, that there are judges of Budgerigars, Canaries and British Birds, who have a sound, practical knowledge of the Foreign exhibits as well, but in my experience they are very much in the minority.

In the case of very small shows, such as Members Only events, I appreciate that economic considerations may necessitate a judge having to double-up on more than one section; but it is only fair to the exhibitors that, at open shows, a competent specialist judge is engaged to assess their entries.

At the present time anyone can describe himself (or herself) as a judge of foreign birds and, if he is appointed to officiate at a show, can allocate the awards according to his opinions. The incompetent judge will probably receive fewer and fewer engagements, and it is unlikely that many show-promoting societies would appoint a judge unless he had been proposed or recommended by one of their members.

Judges' Panels

In an attempt to achieve a degree of uniformity in judging — or at least to improve the overall standard — most specialist societies have established **Judges' Panels**. These constitute a list of judges who have been approved by the specialist society as being competent to undertake the task of judging the Foreign Bird section. At least one specialist society has a number of Judges' Panels, with, at one end of the scale, that for judges who only have seedeater experience, and, at the other, a panel comprising those judges who have had all-round experience with the complete range of species.

Election to these Judges' Panels is based upon the personal reputation of the fancier, which in turn depends largely on his experience in keeping and showing birds in the various categories. In some cases, membership of the specialist society is a prerequisite for election to their Panel of Judges but, in other instances, it is not, and any experienced exhibitor may apply for inclusion in the Panel. Show-promoting societies are not, of course, obliged to appoint a judge from one of the specialist societies' panels unless they are, in fact, applying for the patronage of a particular society. Although most societies in granting patronage stipulate that one of their Panel Judges must be engaged for the event, it can be restrictive if the show committee wish to apply for the patronage of several different societies, unless they can engage a judge who is a member of all the relevant panels. Perhaps a degree of co-operation between the specialist societies could enable a judge, who has been elected to one panel, to become automatically a member of all, provided, of course, that he was experienced with all groups of exotic species. If this idea is a little too optimistic, then at least each specialist society should be prepared to recognise the validity and competence of judges on the panels of the others, from the point of view of patronage allocation.

Although the formation of panels of specialist judges does help to ensure that a reasonable standard of judging is being maintained it is apparent that perhaps more could be achieved in this field. While no one would wish to see Foreign Bird exhibiting become hamstrung by rules and regulations, it seems that a little more formality in the training and election of judges would not be amiss. This is not to suggest that elaborate academic examinations are necessary, but I believe that judges should be called upon to demonstrate that they have a sound practical and theoretical knowledge of their subject. At the same time, trainee judges could be given wider opportunities to study in a practical way under the guidance of recognised experts in their various fields. The present 'system' (or lack of one) is far too disorganised and potential judges learning their future trade by stewarding are liable to pick up as many bad points as good ones.

Stewarding

Acting as steward to a judge is, nevertheless, a useful means of acquiring a working knowledge of the actual methods of judging and many pitfalls can be avoided in this way, particularly if the judge is of a co-operative disposition. One problem, which may occur at shows where the steward is also an exhibitor, is that some show committees will allocate the Foreign Bird exhibitor as a steward to the Canary or Budgerigar judge and vice versa. This practice is not really very helpful if the steward is keen to learn the methods of judging the species which he exhibits.

There does not appear to be much merit in this practice. Presumably the idea is to prevent the steward exercising any influence on the judge when his own birds are being assessed. It seems quite certain that any judge worthy of the title, would not allow himself to be influenced by his steward and, in any case, the vast majority of exhibitors are far too honest to try and obtain an unfair advantage in this way. On the very, very few occasions when one of the exhibitors, acting as steward for me at a show, has stepped out of

10.1 **E. Gallimore of Manchester examines a neat pair of Red-Headed Finches** (*Amadina erythrocephala*) while judging the Foreign Birds at the 1980 **National Exhibition of Cage and Aviary Birds.**

line by deliberately indicating that a particular exhibit belonged to him, his birds have been eliminated from the class and he has been told why this has been done.

In any event, a steward who is an experienced Foreign Bird enthusiast and knows what is required of a good steward, can be of great assistance to the judge, and make his task much easier. Although the judges should check that all the birds in his section have been entered in the correct classes, it is useful if the section steward also carries out this examination so that as little time as possible is lost by having to re-classify wrong entries before the judge can commence his duties. In addition to carrying the show cages from the staging to the judge's bench as and when required, the efficient steward should also arrange for the judging slips to be promptly transferred to the secretary's table. He must also deal with any queries which the judge may have regarding class numbers, patronage nominations or any of the other minor problems which frequently arise during judging. The section steward bears the additional responsibility of ensuring that all the exhibits are adequately fed and watered, and it is therefore obvious that a sound knowledge of exotic species will enable him to carry out his duties more effectively.

The aspiring judge should take every opportunity to act as steward in the Foreign Bird section at as many shows as possible. In this way he will gradually acquire a knowledge of the characteristics of the various species, as well as learning the procedures and methods of a variety of judges. He should also make a point of talking to exhibitors so that he may appreciate some of the problems involved in the management and staging of species, of which he has no personal experience.

TYPICAL SHOW ENGAGEMENT FOR THE JUDGE

In the course of time, the day will dawn when our fancier, having established a reputation as a knowledgeable exhibitor, will be invited to accept an appointment as judge in the Foreign Bird section. As most first engagements are in respect of the smaller shows, the judge will probably be required to deal with all the foreign species which have been entered. In order to forewarn the prospective judge of some of the problems which can arise, and to outline the procedure which I adopt when judging, it may be appropriate if I describe a typical open show engagement.

Arrival at the Show

Several days before the date of the show the judge receives (usually) a copy of the schedule from the show secretary, together with an indication of the time when judging is to commence. This will normally be 10 a.m. but may be earlier in some instances. If there are no navigational directions enclosed with the schedule, the show secretary should be contacted for guidance as it can be most frustrating to arrive at a town in good time, only to be unable to find the show venue, which may often be some obscure church hall completely unknown to most of the local residents.

It is best to arrive at the venue about half an hour before judging is due to start, in order to have a cup of tea, which is usually promptly produced, and meet the section steward and other officials. Incidentally, most societies are very generous in their hospitality towards the judges and some have provided a cooked breakfast on arrival when a long car journey has been involved.

Checking the Entries

The degree of organisation achieved by the show committee before judging commences is prone to vary from show to show. In most cases, however, the show secretary will have prepared the judge's books, specials lists and patronage nominations. The judge's first step is to examine all the exhibits in the Foreign Bird section and check the species in relation to the classification, in order to ensure that no birds have been entered in the wrong class. If any bird is found to be wrongly entered, the show secretary must be informed and the bird transferred to the correct class, with the relevant alterations made to the numbers in the judge's book and the exhibitor's entry form. This latter point is rather important as difficulties may arise, when the fancier tries to pick up his birds at the end of the show, if the alteration to his original entry is overlooked. Some judges do not check for 'wrong classed' birds until they are judging the exhibits, but the difficulty here is that a bird may have to be transferred to a class which has already been judged, with the result that the judge must go back and re-assess that class in order to take account of the additional entry. At the same time as checking that the birds have been correctly entered the judge should also satisfy himself that all the birds are fit to come forward for judging. It occasionally happens that a bird will become unwell after it has been delivered to the show venue — a female may become egg-bound, for example — and if an exhibit is noted which is obviously in such a condition the judge should ask the steward to remove the cage to a warm, quiet situation and eliminate it from the competition.

Judging

Having established that all the exhibits are in correct order, the judge then returns to his stand and asks the steward(s) to bring forward the first class, at the same time telling him the number of exhibits in that class so that no cage is inadvertently overlooked. There may, of course, be only a single entry in the class or there may be twenty or more. In the event of there being only the one

---

10.2 **Blue-Rumped Parrotlets** (*Forpus cyanopygius*)
Not difficult to cater for, they are much less common than the Lovebirds and consequently can do well on the show bench if staged to perfection. The parrotlets of the New World fill the niche occupied in Africa by the Lovebirds. There are a number of similar species, generally green in colour with varying amounts and shades of blue.

10.3 **Red-Headed Finch** (*Amadina erythrocephala*)
A strikingly handsome species from Southern Africa, which may well win the Best in Section. It is frequently available but never in large numbers; quite a hardy species, although females appear to be rather susceptible to egg-binding when breeding. A fine exhibit when in perfect feather for any show team of exotic seedeaters.

exhibit in the class the judge marks a figure '1' on the cage label to indicate that the bird is first and the steward will normally apply an adhesive award label at this time — **red** for first, **blue** for second and **yellow** for third place (where there are sufficient entries, of course).

The exhibit which is placed first, regardless of whether or not it is the only entry in its class, is then set aside, and not returned to the staging, as it will at a later stage be brought forward for consideration when selecting the **Best in Section** for example. It is preferable if these class winners can be accommodated on a side table while awaiting re-appraisal, but circumstances will often dictate that they will have to be placed on the floor, underneath the judging stand. In draughty situations, however, it is advisable to return the exhibits to the staging even if it does mean extra work for the stewards when they have to be retrieved.

In the majority of cases, of course, there will be more than one entry, in each class, and the first seven birds must be placed in order of merit. Although award cards and prize money are generally only awarded for First to Third places in each class, the other four placings are taken into account when assessing points allocation for local or specialist society trophies. Where classes comprise of more than seven entries, the judge should first try and reduce the numbers to more manageable proportions by a process of elimination. This is done by examining the physical condition of each exhibit and discarding all those showing gross defects, such as plucked or badly damaged plumage, missing toes and so on. In a large class there are generally several exhibits which can be eliminated in this way, leaving a 'group' of at least seven entries which are worthy of more detailed examination.

From this point on, only the experience of the judge can really enable him to assess each bird. It is a question of weighing the minor faults of one species against other minor faults of another species, and deciding which should take precedence. It is also at this stage that the judge may appreciate the loneliness of his situation; although there may be many friendly faces close at hand, he cannot turn to any of them for assistance or advice. He can call only on his knowledge to enable him to make his decision and he must be prepared to defend that decision at a later stage to some disgruntled fancier, if the need arises. These decisions can be exceedingly difficult on occasions, but if they are arrived at fairly and in good faith, the vast majority of fanciers will accept them as such. The novice judge cannot, therefore, be told how he must assess the order of merit of six or seven evenly matched individuals of several different species. It is a craft which can only be acquired by experience, and a good judge will continue to expand his knowledge of his subject for the whole of his career.

However large the entry in the Foreign Bird section may be, the judge should always endeavour to carry out his work calmly and unhurriedly. A number of judges can be seen who appear to be in so much of a hurry to keep some other appointment, that they scarcely seem to have the time to examine the exhibits before them. As the exhibitor has probably been involved in considerable expense in getting his birds onto the show bench the least he deserves is that the judge should give them a careful and thorough examination before passing judgement. In any event, the hyper-

active nature of some of the exhibits will require a patient and unflustered approach if the birds are to be seen clearly. It is therefore advisable for the inexperienced judge to take as much time as he needs to examine the entries in detail before marking the placings on the cage labels.

When judging it is wise to carry a red fibre-tip pen, which is ideal for marking on the cage labels, as it is easy to write with and there is no risk of the judge's 'placing' numbers being confused later with the cage numbers already inscribed on the labels by the show secretary. For example, if cage No.1 in Class A is allocated 2nd place, and cage No.2 in the same class is placed first, and both sets of numerals are marked on the cage labels in the same type of ballpoint ink, then errors may well occur when prize cards are being fixed onto the cages, or when the birds are being removed at the end of the show.

Entering the Results

After the cage labels of the seven award winning entries have been marked, the result must be entered in the judge's book. The award columns in the book will be found to be in triplicate with each column perforated vertically; one column is for the use of the person printing the show catalogue (if one is produced), one is for the show secretary's table and the third remains in the judge's book for his reference. It is best to complete all three columns and detach the first two award slips, which are then returned to the show secretary by one of the stewards after each class has been judged, thus minimising any delay in the completion of the paperwork which forms an integral part of every show.

Each class is dealt with in the same way, following the order in which they appear in the schedule, until all the classes in the Foreign Bird section have been judged. The exhibits which have been awarded first place in each class, are then brought forward to compete against each other for the special prizes. In this widely-varying group of species there will probably be several representatives under each of the sub-headings — Common Seedeaters, Rare Seedeaters, Parrot-like and Softbills.

10.4 **Part of the Foreign Bird Section at the 1980 National Exhibition of Cage and Aviary Birds** which was held at Bingley Hall Birmingham. Apart from the competitive element, such events provide a meeting place for thousands of fanciers from all parts of the United Kingdom and Overseas. (Note the all-metal cages in left foreground used to exhibit the larger members of the Parrot family).

Special Awards

Having studied the specials list, which is supplied by the show secretary, and ascertained the exact categories for which prizes have been allocated, the winners of each of the smallest subsections are then selected, progressing upwards by appropriate stages, as the following diagram indicates:

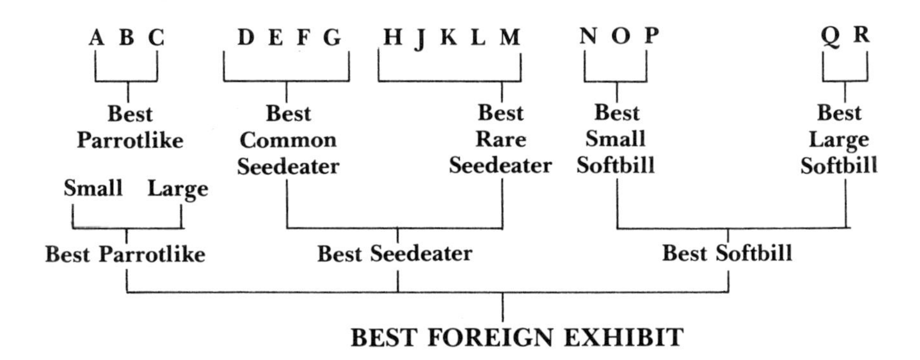

10.5 **Systems of Awards**

Patronage Awards

Although the winners of all the prizes on the **Open Specials** list have now been selected, the judge's task is by no means over. The next step, and often the most frustrating, is to pinpoint the winners of the various patronage awards. When it is remembered that the judge may have to find a **Best Foreign Exhibit** for the patronage awards of seven or eight different local cage bird societies, plus perhaps four national specialist societies, the difficulties of the task may be appreciated. Occasionally, the patron saint of Foreign Bird judges smiles on the event, and to everyone's delight it is found that the bird selected as **Best Foreign Exhibit** in open competition has been nominated for practically every patronage award listed. More often than not, however, this is not the case and the show secretary's efficiency then plays a critical role in the proceedings. Hopefully, he will have prepared a sheet with a headed column for each society which has granted patronage to the Foreign Bird section, and entered in these columns will be the class and cage numbers of each exhibit which has been nominated for the patronage awards of the appropriate society. The cage number of the **Best Foreign**

Exhibit can then be checked against this list. This procedure will generally provide the winner of some of the patronage awards.

In selecting the **Best Foreign Exhibit** the judge will normally have placed the leading contenders into order of merit, at least in his mind if not actually on paper. The numbers of the exhibits, which he knows to be second and third Best Foreign, should also be checked against the list of patronage nominations, and in this way some of the other patronage award winners can often be identified.

It will sometimes be necessary, however, for those birds which have been nominated for a particular patronage to be brought forward and judged together as a class in order to find the overall winner. Where a large number of entries is involved, this may seem to be a rather cumbersome procedure, but it is the only fair method of finding the patronage award winners. In any event, as the judge will already have examined all the exhibits thoroughly while selecting the open prize winners, he will be able to discard immediately those with serious faults thereby reducing his 'patronage classes' to reasonable proportions.

It is, of course, only possible to select patronage award winners fairly and efficiently if the show secretary has prepared a full and complete list of all the entries which have been nominated under the relevant headings. Without such a list, judging conditions can become chaotic and therefore all secretaries are entreated to ensure that they have attended to this additional, but essential, chore before the judging is due to commence.

In the case of some of the lesser patronages— particularly those of some of the local cage bird societies— it frequently occurs that the only birds nominated are those which have been placed fourth or even lower in their respective classes. Although it may appear to be rather ludicrous that a bird, which has only achieved fifth or sixth place in its class, has it cage adorned with a rosette inscribed *Anytown C.B.S. — Best Foreign Exhibit*, the award must be given provided that the patronage conditions of the *Anytown C.B.S.* permit. It is becoming increasingly more prevalent, however, that local cage bird societies are stipulating that their patronage awards are to be granted to First Prize winners only. In those cases where the 'class winners only' stipulation applies to a particular patronage, the fact should be noted clearly by the show secretary on the judge's patronage list.

Whether or not this requirement is practically sound, is open to

debate. It certainly makes the judge's task simpler and in some cases it could be argued that it enhances the value of the award. There are, however, many occasions when the bird, which is second or even third in its class, is vastly superior to those which have been placed first in their respective classes. It is indeed often true to say that it is preferable to be second in a class of twenty birds than first in a class of one! In such cases, of course, the exhibit receiving the patronage award would not be the best of those nominated, but only the best of those eligible on account of the patronage restriction.

However efficient the show organisation may be, patronage awards certainly create a considerable amount of additional work and complications for the judge and show organisers alike. As I have suggested elsewhere, the advantages which many of these patronage allocations bestow are of doubtful validity in terms of the success of the show, and show-promoting societies would be well advised to consider the question of patronage carefully, before seeking more than they can adequately cope with on the day of the show.

Best Exhibit in Show

When the judge has finally selected all the patronage award winners and all the judging slips and award sheets have been returned to the secretary's table, he will find, at some shows, that he still has one task to complete. This is, of course, to select the **Best Exhibit in Show**. Many societies have, thankfully, discarded this award as it is in some ways rather meaningless, but others still persist and it is probably true to say that it accounts for more animosity between judges than any other aspect of exhibiting.

It is scarcely surprising, of course, that disputes arise when four or five judges are each comparing the merits of the best bird in their favourite section with those of the top birds in sections which may be quite unfamiliar to them. In my own case, for example, in addition to being a regular judge of the Foreign, Bengalese and Zebra Finch sections, I have in the past kept and exhibited Budgerigars and British Birds. Although this gives me, therefore,

10.6 **Black Lory** (*Chalcopsittacus ater*)
A beautiful show bird. Occasionally available in this country, this strikingly handsome species is more suitable for the experienced aviculturist. It is a native of New Guinea.

a reasonable knowledge of the essential good points of these two last-named groups, I would certainly not profess to have the width of experience necessary to pass fair judgement on a class of either variety. Similarly in the case of Canaries, which I have kept but never exhibited, I am familiar with the general standards of the different varieties, but have never had the inclination or opportunity to learn of their finer points.

It would, therefore, be quite unfair to the exhibitor if I were to attempt to judge a class of Budgerigars, Canaries or British Birds, but yet I am asked to pass judgment on these varieties while selecting the Supreme Award winner at many shows. In the same way, of course, the **Best Foreign Bird** is also being assessed for this award by the other judges, some of whom at least will not even be capable of identifying the species. This is why it is suggested that this award is rather meaningless and its allocation will often be decided by the judge who has the strongest personality or loudest voice. Even on those occasions when all the judges involved give a fair and honest assessment of the bird they have put forward as best in their respective sections, it is still extremely difficult to compare the relative merits of the different varieties objectively.

APPENDIX

Importation of Birds into Great Britain

Although the majority of aviculturists, who keep exotic species, obtain their birds from other breeders or professional dealers in this country, some do import stock from breeders on the Continent, or direct from commercial trappers in the country of origin. It may, therefore, be useful to explain the current situation relating to the importation of birds into this country.

CONTROLS

Until fairly recently there were virtually no controls affecting foreign bird imports associated with disease prevention. A ban on the importation of Parrot–like birds designed to reduce the incidence of *Psittacosis* was subsequently revoked.

However, the importation of all birds into Great Britain is now strictly controlled by the **Importation of Birds, Poultry and Hatching Eggs Order 1979**. This legislative instrument was enacted in an effort to reduce the risk of bird diseases, such as Newcastle Disease, being introduced into this country and thereafter transmitted to commercial poultry.

The Order has the effect of prohibiting the importation of virtually all birds except under a licence issued by the appropriate Government Department or Ministry. The restrictions also apply to hatching eggs, of course, as the title of the Order suggests and this should be borne in mind by those aviculturists who might wish to import eggs of Pheasants, Quail, Jungle Fowl, Wild Fowl, and so on with a view to hatching them in incubators or under bantam foster–parents.

IMPORT LICENCE

It should be noted that it is essential to obtain an import licence well in advance of the actual date of importation, and before the licence is issued it will be necessary for the Ministry to be satisfied with all the relevant arrangements.

The first step, therefore, having located an overseas supplier of the birds one requires, is to obtain an application form (Form IM 62) from the appropriate Government office. This will depend on which region of Great Britain the birds are to be imported into and will therefore be one of the following:–

For England	**Ministry of Agriculture, Fisheries and Food,** **Animal Health Division (Import Section)** **Hook Rise South** **Tolworth** **Surbiton** **Surrey** **KT6 7NF**
For Scotland	**Department of Agriculture and Fisheries for Scotland** **Animal Welfare Branch** **Chesser House** **500 Gorgie Road** **Edinburgh EH11 3AW**
For Wales	**Welsh Office Agriculture Department** **Park Avenue** **Aberystwyth** **Dyfed** **SY23 1PQ**

It should also be noted that if one proposes importing (or exporting) any species of Bird of Prey or endangered species of bird, it will be necessary to obtain a special licence under the **Endangered Species (Import and Export) Act 1976**. The licensing requirements of this particular legislation are administered by the Department of the Environment to whom relevant applications should be made at Tollgate House, Houlton Street, Bristol BS2 9DJ.

Application forms, when duly completed, should be returned to the appropriate office at least one month prior to the anticipated date of import and preferably longer to allow for any queries which may arise.

Types of import licence

There are, in fact, three different categories of import licence, defined according to the types and numbers of birds and other factors, as follows:–

1. **Twelve bird Licence**: this permits the importation of up to

twelve birds (or hatching eggs) from those countries where the poultry disease situation is regarded as satisfactory. The birds to be imported must have been in captivity for at least twenty–eight days before importation and must be accompanied by a veterinary health certificate. This health certificate, on the prescribed form IM 67, must be completed by an official veterinary surgeon specifically authorised for the purpose by the Government of the exporting country.

2. **Non-psittacine Licence**: allows the importation of an unlimited number of non-Parrot–like species or their hatching eggs (or up to 100 exhibition type poultry or their hatching eggs). As with the previous category of licence, the imported birds must be accompanied by an official veterinary health certificate, although the form of the certificate differs from the previous one, being now required on prescribed form IM 120. It should be noted that, with this type of licence, there is no requirement that the birds must have been in captivity for any stipulated period before importation. However, the veterinary surgeon must certify that no cases of Newcastle Disease or fowl plague have been diagnosed on the premises of origin during the previous six weeks. The birds to be imported must, as with all three categories of licence, be examined by the veterinarian not *earlier* than seven days prior to the proposed date of export.
3. **Full Quarantine Licence**: required for all importations of birds and hatching eggs not covered by the previous two categories of licence, for example consignments of more than twelve Parrot–like birds.

IMPORTATION STANDARDS

Most consignments of exotic birds are now transported to this country by air, as this method subjects the birds to less stress and for a much shorter period. In the fairly recent past, there have been a number of unfortunate incidents involving the import of foreign species, where considerable numbers of birds have been found to be dead or dying on arrival at the airport of entry. These tragic cases have often been the result of overcrowding and/or inadequate containers arising from ignorance or lack of concern on the part of the exporter or his agents.

Containers for livestock importation must now comply with the appropriate standards prescribed by the **International Air Transport Association**, full details of which can be obtained from the airline on whose aircraft the birds will be carried.

Airlines, or other shippers, will also require evidence that an appropriate import licence has been issued, before they will accept consignments of birds for transportation to Great Britain. When an import licence has been issued by the relevant Ministry or Department of Government, they will also issue a Boarding Permit, which must be forwarded to the exporter or his agent, and produced by him as evidence to the shipper that a licence has been issued.

Personal importation
Aviculturists, who propose holidaying on the Continent of Europe, or elsewhere overseas, may feel tempted to combine pleasures by visiting private breeders or dealers in the country visited with a view to obtaining fresh blood or some of the scarcer species for their collections. It is sometimes practicable under these circumstances, if travelling by car, to bring back the birds personally, but acquisitions of birds in this way cannot be a spontaneous undertaking and require careful forward planning. The number and species of birds to be imported and the name and address of the exporter must be known in advance, as this information must be contained in the application for the import licence. It should be noted that the method of transport of any consignment of imported birds from the port or airport of entry to their quarantine premises must also be given in the application, and that the use of public transport for this purpose is not permissible.

CONTROL ON PREMISES

One of the most important factors involved in the issue of a bird import licence is the provision of suitable premises in which the birds will be confined after importation. The premises must be inspected and approved by a veterinary officer appointed by the appropriate Agriculture Department, before the licence is issued.

Two categories of premises are recognised and these are related to the type of licence.

1. **Quarantine Premises**: must be suitable for birds imported under a Full Quarantine Licence. In rural areas such premises must be located at a distance of at least half-a-mile from any concentration of poultry or other birds. In urban situations a lesser degree of separation may be approved at the Ministry's discretion. In either case, no domestic poultry or other birds are permitted to be on the quarantine premises.

2. **Isolation Premises**: Premises in this category may be used for the isolation of birds imported under Non-psittacine or twelve bird licences. The premises must not contain any commercial poultry and approval will depend on the type and numbers of domestic poultry or other birds on the premises and in the vicinity.

In addition to considering the actual location of the premises the Veterinary Inspector will also have to be satisfied with regard to the general suitability of the accommodation and equipment. Factors which will be taken into account in assessing the premises will include:

1. **Capability of being effectively cleaned and disinfected**
2. **Security against the escape of the imported birds and the entry of wild birds**
3. **Proof against the entry of vermin**
4. **Need for specialised environments or requirements of certain species if necessary**
5. **Adequate ventilation control**
6. **Adequate water supply for drinking and cleansing**
7. **Adequate drainage including ensuring that it is not accessible to birds outside the premises**
8. **Storage and removal of excreta and litter**
9. **Food storage — capacity and proof against birds and vermin**
10. **Adequacy of lighting for inspection of the birds**
11. **Adequate heating facilities for the species concerned**
12. **Suitability and provision of protective clothing and footwear for attendants and authorised visitors**
13. **Refrigerator facilities for holding dead birds prior to despatch to laboratory in the case of premises with a large throughput of imported birds**

Control Birds

In the case of Full Quarantine importations, provision must be made for maintaining three four to eight week–old chickens as control birds in the quarantine premises. The three chickens (unvaccinated) must be placed in the premises prior to the arrival of the imported birds and must give a negative result to a Haemagglutination Inhibition test for Newcastle Disease not more than fourteen days before the commencement of the quarantine period. A similar test is carried out after twenty eight days of the quarantine period have elapsed. Control birds are not required in the case of twelve-bird importations, but may, in some instances, be specified for certain consignments of birds imported under a Non–psittacine Licence.

QUARANTINE

It should be noted that, in the case of isolation premises, that is for twelve-bird and Non–psittacine importations, it is not a prerequisite that the consignment (or amalgamation of consignments) forming the quarantine group of imported birds shall be the sole avian occupants of the establishment. It is, however, stipulated that the imported birds must be kept separate from any other birds housed on the same premises. This can, presumably, be achieved by accommodating the birds in different cages or flights, but it is obviously preferable that the imported birds should be housed in a quite separate room.

The normal period of quarantine or isolation is thirty-five days from the date the imported birds are brought into the premises. If the quarantine group is to comprise of more than one consignment, then the thirty-five day period will commence with the arrival of the final consignment, although the quarantine conditions will apply from the date of arrival of the first birds. In the case of imported eggs, these must be hatched in the quarantine or isolation premises, with the chicks thereafter remaining in the premises for a thirty-five-day period. The thirty-five-day period may be extended in the event of disease occurring or being detected during the quarantine period.

Alternatively, the Agriculture Department may require the imported birds to be re–exported or slaughtered without compensation, depending on the particular circumstances of the disease incident.

Any imported birds found to be sick or dead during the quarantine period must be referred to the Veterinary Inspector for pathological or post–mortem examination, and no birds, either dead or alive, must be removed from the premises without the official written authorisation of the Ministry's Divisional Veterinary Officer.

All expenses arising from the requirements relating to the quarantine or isolation of imported birds must be met by the importer. These expenses also include the fees of the Local Veterinary Inspector, appointed by the Ministry, for all visits to the quarantine or isolation premises. The importer must also ensure that he has obtained any necessary planning or building regulation consent for the quarantine or isolation premises, including possible approval for change of use.

Concessions

There are a number of relatively minor concessions, which have been covered by the issue of general licences by the Ministry as follows:

1. Unrestricted imports of birds into the United Kingdom is permitted from Northern Ireland, the Republic of Ireland, the Isle of Man and the Channel Islands.
2. Up to two pet birds may be imported, if accompanied by their owner, who must also sign a declaration to H.M. Customs and Excise at the port of entry. The pet birds must have been in the owner's possession in captivity for at least two months (or since hatching if younger than two months) and the owner must undertake to keep the birds in isolation for thirty-five days at an address specified on the declaration. No other birds or live poultry must be kept at that address, and the birds must be made available for inspection by a representative of the appropriate Agriculture Department.
   This concession does not apply to any pet birds which fall into the category of poultry. For this purpose, poultry is defined as fowls, turkeys, geese, ducks, guinea fowls, pheasants, partridges and quails.
3. Consignments of birds and hatching eggs may be landed at a port or airport in this country, provided they are re–exported from that port within a period of forty-eight hours. Where imported birds are landed at one airport in Great Britain and are to be re–exported from another airport elsewhere in the country, they may be transferred between the two airports by aircraft.
4. Up to two pet birds may be imported into Great Britain for onward transportation to Northern Ireland, provided that

the owner is in possession of a valid import licence issued by the Department of Agriculture for Northern Ireland and a veterinary health certificate, and can sign the appropriate declaration and undertaking to H.M. Customs and Excise.

5. Import licences with special conditions may be issued by the appropriate Agriculture Department to professional entertainers who use birds as part of their acts.

Bibliography

BUCHAN, J. *The Bengalese Finch*, Isles d'Avon Bristol 1976

FORSHAW, J.M. and COOPER, W.T. *Parrots of the World*, Landsdowne Press, Melbourne 1973

ILES, G. *Breeding Australian Finches*, Isles d'Avon, Bristol 1976

IMMELMANN, K. *Australian Finches in Bush and Aviary*, Angus and Robertson, Sydney 1965

KING, B., WOODCOCK, M. and DICKINSON, E.C. *Birds of South-East Asia*, Collins, London 1975

PROZESKY, O.P.M. *Birds of Southern Africa*, Collins, London 1970

RESTALL, R. *Finches and Other Seedeaters*, Faber and Faber, London 1975

ROOTS, C. *Softbilled Birds*, John Gifford, London 1970

RUTGERS, A. *Handbook of Foreign Birds*, Blandford Press, London 1964

SMITH, G.A. *Lovebirds and Related Parrots*, Paul Elek, London 1979

Index

WIDENER UNIVERSITY
WOLFGRAM
LIBRARY
CHESTER, PA.

DATE DUE